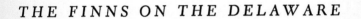

THE FINNS ON THE DELAWARE

ADMIRAL KLAS FLEMING

Director of the New Sweden Company, 1637-1644
From a painting in The Law Courts, Stockholm

THE
FINNS ON THE
DELAWARE

1638-1655

An Essay in American Colonial History

JOHN H. WUORINEN
ASSISTANT PROFESSOR OF HISTORY
COLUMBIA UNIVERSITY

NEW YORK   MORNINGSIDE HEIGHTS

COLUMBIA UNIVERSITY PRESS

1938

Copyright 1938

COLUMBIA UNIVERSITY PRESS, NEW YORK

Foreign agents: OXFORD UNIVERSITY PRESS, Humphrey Milford, Amen House, London, E.C. 4, England, AND B. I. Building, Nicol Road, Bombay, India; KWANG HSUEH PUBLISHING HOUSE, 140 Peking Road, Shanghai, China; MARUZEN COMPANY, LTD., 6 Nihonbashi, Tori-Nichome, Tokyo, Japan

MANUFACTURED IN THE UNITED STATES OF AMERICA

PREFACE

EVER since Th. Campanius Holm published, in 1702, a Swedish description of New Sweden, the subject has periodically attracted a variety of writers. During the past century the story has been told time and again, and the number of books and more-or-less substantial articles dealing with it is considerable. It was not until 1911, when Dr. Amandus Johnson published his *The Swedish Settlements on the Delaware, 1638-1664*, that the first full-length history in the field appeared. Basing his description upon thorough research at home and abroad, Dr. Johnson produced a work of impressive proportions. Its very size, however, tends to obscure for the ordinary reader some of the essential features of Sweden-Finland's seventeenth-century experiment in American colonization. The book is in a way a valuable collection of sources rather than a clear and connected narrative. Indispensable to students of New Sweden history, it has probably been extensively used by every writer who has dealt with the Swedes and Finns on the Delaware during the past quarter century.

The present study owes its existence primarily to the fact that the Tercentenary of the Delaware settlements is to be celebrated this year. Under the circumstances it seemed desirable to publish a description, in the form of a brief summary, of the New Sweden colony and the Finnish aspects of the enterprise. As the title indicates, the story covers only the years when New Sweden existed. Excepting occasional references to the period after 1655, no attempt has been made to extend the narrative beyond the chronological limits indicated by the seventeen years during which the Swedish flag flew on the Delaware.

I am indebted to Dr. Amandus Johnson for permission to quote from *The Swedish Settlements on the Delaware, 1638-1664*, to Charles Scribner's Sons for permission to quote from Albert Cook Myers (ed.), *Narratives of Early Pennsylvania, West New Jersey and Delaware, 1630-1707*, and to Columbia University Press for the right to include materials which have previously appeared in my *Nationalism in Modern Finland*. I am likewise under obligation to Mr. John H. Bourne, of the Federal Writers' Project, Works Progress Administration, New Jersey, for permission to quote from the forthcoming volume *The Swedes and Finns in New Jersey*, ably

PREFACE

prepared by Mrs. Irene Fuhlbruegge. Finally, it is my pleasant duty to record that the publication of this book has been made possible by the financial grant generously made by the American Finnish Delaware Tercentenary Committee.

JOHN H. WUORINEN

Columbia University
May 15, 1938

CONTENTS

[ix]

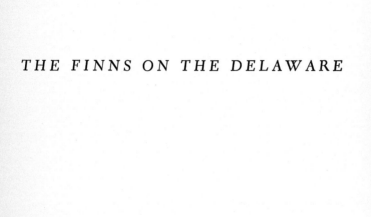

THE FINNS ON THE DELAWARE

I

THE BACKGROUND

ON A day in March in the year 1638 two ships carrying a flag strange to American waters sailed up the Delaware River. The ships hailed from the far-away Swedish kingdom. Months earlier they had left their home port in search of the riches and opportunity which the New World had held out to the Old ever since the Spaniard had begun to exploit his colonies more than a century earlier. A few decades before the arrival of the two ships which were winding their way up the Delaware, English and Dutch builders of empires colonial and commercial had established themselves on these shores. To their ventures there would now be added another, under the Swedish flag.

The newcomers landed on the river shore where present-day Wilmington stands. Tradition has it that they named the place Paradise Point.

During the generation preceding the arrival of the New Sweden pioneers on the Delaware River, Sweden-Finland had come to occupy a new position in the family of European states.[1] Having been, earlier, an unimportant state far removed from the main orbit of European affairs, it had become one of the leading arbiters of the destinies of the Continent. Before the year 1630 the conquests of the southern littoral of the Baltic had resulted in the inclusion of a substantial part of the Baltic provinces within the boundaries of the kingdom. By the middle of the seventeenth century, participation in the Thirty Years' War had not only brought territory in Germany but great influence and prestige as well. Especially in the eyes of Protestant Europe, Sweden had come to stand forth as the savior of the cause for which Luther, Melanchthon, and

---

1. In recent years historians in Sweden and Finland have begun to use the term "Sweden-Finland" when writing on periods or topics that relate to the Swedish kingdom as a whole down to the year 1809, when Finland, the eastern part of the kingdom, was annexed by Russia. For instance, see Eli F. Heckscher, *Sverges ekonomiska historia*, Vol. I (Stockholm, 1935-1936), *passim*. The designation is useful in that it brings to mind what the Swedish kingdom comprised during the many centuries that Sweden and Finland constituted a single state. It likewise distinguishes between the kingdom proper on the one hand and the provinces temporarily held by Sweden-Finland along the southern coasts of the Baltic Sea on the other.

others had done battle a century earlier. The power and prestige thus won sustained Sweden-Finland until the wars of Charles XII (1697-1718) brought the kingdom to the brink of ruin and prepared the ground for serious territorial and other losses in the future.

By the time the Thirty Years' War placed the Swedish kingdom in the forefront of European nations, Finland had been a part of Sweden for more than four hundred years.

The so-called "Swedish conquest" of Finland began about the middle of the twelfth century and was completed by the close of the thirteenth. The conquest was more a provincial Uppland undertaking than an enterprise carried out by a unified state, for at that time Sweden was not as yet a unified kingdom. It consisted of a number of confederated provinces, each of which had its own laws, judge, and assembly (landsting). These provincial assemblies were the only lawmaking bodies then in existence, and their laws and customs had no binding force beyond their own limits. Through their "law-man" they participated in the election of the common king, who had to obtain confirmation of his election from the various provincial assemblies, whose laws he agreed to observe.

Thus a centralized state had not yet come into being at the time when Finland became a part of the kingdom. That Finland became a part of Sweden centuries before the process of national unification had destroyed the province as the basic unit of political organization was of fundamental importance to Finland and the Finns. Finland's position in the kingdom and many of the basic aspects of the later institutional development of the country can be understood only in the light of the fact that the Swedes and the Finns were brought under a common roof centuries before concepts of law, administrative practices, political authority, and the like had come to have a clearly defined meaning outside and independent of the province.

The political and legal rights of Finland's inhabitants were the same as those enjoyed by the Swedes; Swedes and Finns possessed the same prerogatives. Both participated, through their representatives, in the election of the king while the elective kingship lasted (till the reign of Gustavus Vasa (1523-1560). As regards positions in the service of State or Church, the Finns were "native Swedes." Nor was representation in the *Riksdag* ever denied them. The *Riksdagsordning* of 1617 and later laws which established the *Riksdag* and defined its composition, functions, and powers provided for representation of Sweden and Finland alike. The same qualifications for the right to vote, eligibility to seats in the *Riksdag*, and method of selecting members prevailed in both sections of the kingdom.[2] As early as the close of the thirteenth century the Catholic Church had become firmly established, and "Swedish law" had come to be applied throughout the country—incidentally, the first common code of law for the provinces of Sweden proper had been completed some fifty years earlier—and Finland had come to occupy, one might say, the position of one of the several provinces of which the kingdom was composed.

When later centralization began to gain ground at the expense of local institutions, the provinces grew into a larger, more compact unit. The process may be said to have been completed by Gustavus Vasa (1523-1560), who established a hereditary monarchy and whose successful personal rule contributed national organs of law and administration.

---

2. See *Historiallinen arkisto*, XIII (1894), 1-79, and E. G. Palmén, *Suomen valtiopäiväin historia* (1910), Pt. 1. Strictly speaking, considerable diversity in the manner of election existed in the various localities in the Swedish and Finnish parts of the realm.

Yet nothing illustrates more clearly the gradualness of the changes that were taking place than the fact that it was not until 1617 that the Estates of the Realm, in Riksdag assembled, obtained recognition in law. In other words, the Swedish kingdom may be said to have become a centralized monarchy only a few decades before the arrival of the Swedish and Finnish colonists in the New World.[3]

The developments and circumstances outlined above seem to have been responsible for the absence of that antagonism between the Swedes and the Finns which often appears when two linguistic groups are brought into close contact and under the same political authority. But it is safe to say that other factors were no less important. The Finns and the Swedes had not been separated before the twelfth century. Swedish-speaking inhabitants had lived in Finland centuries earlier, and that trade between Finland and Sweden had been carried on from early times has been amply demonstrated. Furthermore, no profound differences existed in the culture of the two groups or in the stage of social development reached by them. Nor did the con-

---

3. I have summarized the developments sketched in these paragraphs in my *Nationalism in Modern Finland* (New York, 1931), ch. i; see also *ibid.*, pp. 42-47.

quest of the twelfth century mean the discovery of regions particularly suited for material exploitation. The backwardness of the economic development of Sweden, the absence of a strong, centralized government, and the lack of valuable natural resources in sparsely populated Finland appear to account for the absence of economic exploitation as a concomitant of the conquest. Hence, prejudices and antipathies found but poor soil in which to grow, and economic interest had no appreciable chance to strengthen them.

By the seventeenth century Finland had become, not a subject province of Sweden, but an integral part of the kingdom, whose inhabitants were "native Swedes" in the eyes of the law, possessing the same rights and privileges as were enjoyed by the inhabitants of the Swedish part of the kingdom. Law and the administration of justice, religious life, education, and governmental and administrative organization were institutionalized in both parts of the kingdom according to patterns which had been gradually evolved in the course of a common history extending over several centuries.[4]

---

4. This statement applies to the whole period of more than six hundred years which was brought to a close in 1808-1809, when Finland was conquered by Russia and

The colony of New Sweden on the Delaware began its history during the early years of Sweden-Finland's newly won renown and position in Europe. But however much the establishment of the colony was influenced by the fact that the kingdom had become one of the leading powers of that day, its founding and especially its subsequent development were more dependent upon the general economic and other basic aspects of the monarchy than upon the extent to which military exploits, diplomatic triumphs, and territorial gains accompanied the statesmanship of Gustavus Adolphus and his successors. In other words, the population, the economic and other resources of the kingdom, the extent of her trade and commerce were of more basic significance in determining the nature and results of the Swedish experiment in colonial empire building in America than the achievements which left the names of Gustavus Adolphus, Oxenstierna, Fleming, Baner, Torstensson, and Stalhandske on the pages of seventeenth-century European history.

The question concerning the population of Sweden-Finland during the first half of the seventeenth century admits of no definite answer. Popu-

---

transformed into an autonomous, self-governing Grand-Duchy in union with the Russian Empire.

lation statistics for the period are nonexistent, of course; it was not until 1751 that Sweden-Finland began systematically to record the population of the country. The best available estimates indicate, however, that the figure 1,000,000 probably represents an acceptable approximation.[5] Of this number probably 95 percent were rural, and even the urban population, estimated at 5 percent, was in all likelihood more dependent upon agrarian pursuits than the classification "urban" suggests. For all practical purposes, therefore, Sweden-Finland may be said to have been, during the period of the Thirty Years' War, nearly wholly an agrarian kingdom.

In speaking of the economic aspects of the kingdom some two generations before the New Sweden enterprise was begun, the leading Swedish economic historian remarks that markedly primitive conditions prevailed and suggests that in order to find a corresponding level of development in Western Europe, one would perhaps have to go back beyond the year 1000 A.D.[6] By the closing decades of

5. See Eli F. Heckscher, op. cit., Vol. I, ch. i, and Amandus Johnson, The Swedish Settlements on the Delaware, 1638-1664 (Philadelphia, 1911), p. 31. This figure represents roughly one-tenth of the combined population of Finland and Sweden in our day.

6. Ibid., I, 32.

the sixteenth century, however, it had become evident that several trends were at work changing the old and ushering in the new. Money economy was replacing barter economy, and exploitation of the Swedish iron and other mineral resources (which have long since become outstandingly important in the national economy of Sweden), increase in trade and commerce, with consequent growth in the number and importance of cities, the taking up of new lands for cultivation in some of the frontier regions of Sweden-Finland which had hitherto marked the limits of settled communities within the kingdom were all beginning to spell the destruction of the primitive state of earlier days and to furnish the bases of a monarchy even more closely patterned on the models furnished by the rising "modern" national monarchies of England, France, and other countries. Mercantilist economic policy and administrative centralization are conspicuous evidences of the "modernization" of the Swedish monarchy during the whole century that preceded the arrival in the New World of the first expedition from the kingdom, in 1638.

Among the developments that spelled important change in the economic life of Sweden-Finland, three deserve passing mention, especially because they relate, directly or indirectly, to the New Sweden colony and its history. The first refers to changes in Swedish agriculture which took place approximately during 1580-1650. The area under cultivation was considerably extended, especially in the region from the Värmland province to Angermanland.

Perhaps the most conspicuous phase of this agrarian frontier pioneering and apparently the one which has been most definitely recorded was the emigration of settlers from Finland to central and western Sweden, there to take up lands which hitherto had been touched neither by the woodsman's axe nor the farmer's plow.

The emigration of Finns to Sweden commenced in the 1580's and continued down to about 1700. The main period of the emigration fell between 1580 and 1650. It began at the instance of public authority desirous of bringing new lands under the plow and ultimately became, as one Swedish historian puts it, "incomparably the most systematic" pioneering enterprise within Sweden during the sixteen hundreds.[7] According to estimates, it involved some 12,000-13,000 persons, who left their home-

7. *Ibid.*, I, 396.

steads in Finland in the search for new opportunity in the Swedish part of the kingdom. That the emigration was, relatively, of large dimensions is suggested by the fact that the number of persons involved was probably as great as the total urban population of the kingdom during that period.[8]

At the time when the emigration of the Finns to Sweden was beginning to mark the carving of new settlements out of the wilderness in central and western Sweden, the technique of exploiting the resources of the soil was but little developed. So-called modern methods of agriculture, diversification of crops, drainage, fertilization, and the like were unknown throughout Europe until the eighteenth century and later, and it was not until the nineteenth century that they began appreciably to affect

---

8. The Finnish settlers went to Värmland, especially the northern part of Värmland, Södermanland, and spread over a continuous territory from the Norwegian border over Narke and Western Dalarne and Orsa; they were likewise found in Gästriksland and Ångermanland. See *ibid.*, p. 396. It should be noted that homesteading was not limited to the Finns, although their contribution to this phase of Sweden's development stands out in many ways more conspicuously and has left a more marked impression than has corresponding pioneering on the part of the Swedes. See *ibid.*, p. 137.

the life and labor of the Swedish and the Finnish farmers. In the sixteenth and seventeenth centuries they wrested a living from a niggardly soil by adhering to time-honored ways of clearing land, sowing the seed, and harvesting the crops, which were all too often anything but abundant.

Of basic importance with respect to the farming of that distant period was the method of clearing forest land for arable land. It consisted of felling the trees and cutting the underbrush—usually in the autumn—and setting fire to it in the spring. At relatively little labor the homesteader thus gained a twofold advantage: the clearing of the land and an increased yield of the land, for the ashes served to add to the fertility of the soil. After hoeing or superficial plowing, sowing took place, and in due time a crop was harvested where the forest had previously held undisputed sway.

This method appears to have been common in Sweden-Finland, especially in the frontier regions of the kingdom, where forest land was abundant. It tended to spell extensive rather than intensive cultivation, in that the farmer appears often to have moved on to a new potential clearing as soon as soil exhaustion began to limit the yield of the old.

In spite of the wastefulness of the method, it was

approved and encouraged by the authorities. For instance, the inhabitants of the Värmland province (one of the provinces to which the Finnish settlers were beginning to move about the year 1580) were ordered in 1587 to clear yearly enough land by burning to add about an acre to the land already under cultivation. "The objective was that the Finns should move from place to place, to cultivate a plot of ground for a year or two, and then take up new land." [9] For some fifty years, or down to the 1630's, the Finnish pioneers of central and western Sweden added to the cultivated area of these sections of the kingdom by means of the farming technique briefly described, and in doing so they were aided and encouraged by provincial authority as well as by edicts of the Crown. Ultimately, however, the wastefulness of the method and other circumstances led to a change of policy and the formulation of increasingly strict prohibitions against the continued destruction of the forest resources of the country.

The second development related to the rise of the mining industry. The prohibitions and the penalties

---

9. *Ibid.*, p. 399. This account of farming techniques and of its consequences is largely based on the material presented by Heckscher in Book II, ch. i.

which accompanied them were directed against all and sundry who practiced the method of clearing land mentioned above, particularly against the Finns, who used it more conspicuously and extensively than did their Swedish neighbors. Thus an edict of 1636 was applied primarily to them. Harsh punishment was meted out to those who failed to observe the demands of the law. In 1638 and again in 1639 measures were formulated for the purpose of saving the forests, and the Regency called the attention of provincial governors to the losses caused by the Finns, which, it was maintained, "amounted to millions." In 1664 an ordinance provided the death penalty for the second offense and stated that Finns guilty of breaking the ordinance should be driven from their farms, that their property and crops should be destroyed, and that they should be jailed or deported to New Sweden. The problem of how to prevent the farmers from following the custom of clearing land by cutting down and burning the forests continued to vex Riksdag and Crown for decades, until forest ordinances with increasingly severe penalties and perhaps other circumstances also appear to have reduced it to more manageable dimensions in the early part of the eighteenth century.

Several factors account for the change in policy during the generation beginning about 1630. With particular reference to the Finnish homesteaders, the following circumstances should be noted. When the Crown began to encourage frontier settlements in hitherto uncultivated parts of Sweden, special privileges were granted to the immigrants from Finland and others willing to assume the rôle of pioneering in the wilderness. They were granted, for instance, freedom from taxation for periods ranging up to ten years. It was expected, however, that the farmers thus temporarily favored would in due time swell the ranks of the taxpaying agrarian population. This expectation often did not materialize, especially in the case of those Finns who for some reason either could not or would not become settled farmers but who preferred to lead lives in which hunting, fishing, and "migratory farming" perhaps played equally important parts.

Then, too, the forests of the country, though abundant, were growing in importance, and wasteful exploitation was more objectionable than in earlier days. They had been used since time immemorial as common lands for hunting and grazing, gathering of firewood, and the like. In the late sixteenth century and the first half of the seventeenth they assumed a new significance because of the expansion of the mining industry, both iron and copper. Thus the pioneer who cleared his land by cutting the forest and burning it frequently got into difficulties with farmers who felt that time-honored hunting, grazing, and other rights were being violated by the newcomers. More important still, the frontiersman got into difficulties with the mining interests of the day, whose enterprises were often identified by the Crown with the vital interests of the kingdom as a whole. A twofold opposition to the Finns was the result, and they were forced to yield to the demands especially of the mining industry, a new and significant factor in the national economy of Sweden from the seventeenth century onward.

While the presence of abundant and exceptionally pure iron ore, and copper ore also, had brought mining into being in Sweden long before the period dealt with in this chapter, it was only in the seventeenth century that Sweden became an important producer of iron, and one hundred years later Sweden was, for a time, the leading producer of this important commodity. In the sixteen hundreds Sweden rose temporarily to the position of the largest European producer of copper. Neither of these significant developments in the economic life of the country could have taken place in the absence of wood for charcoal; the need of the mining industry for charcoal was the fundamental reason for the change in the policy toward the use of forests observed above, and therefore, as already noted, came to play a decisive part in changing the conditions under which the Finnish settlers, especially, lived.

Before turning to still another development which affected the economic aspects of Sweden-Finland during the decades before and after 1638 and which is consequently related to the broad background of the New Sweden venture in colonial enterprise, a final observation regarding the frontier pioneering discussed above should be made.

It would be misleading to imply that the majority of the Finnish pioneers in central Sweden belonged to the group of "migratory farmers" exposed to the prohibitions and penalties of the increasingly exacting forest and other ordinances. In many localities they established permanent farms or became part of the rising mining communities and came to play important parts in the development of the new industry. For instance, in western Västmanland the Ljusnaberg copper mine was discovered by a Finn, in 1624. Eleven years later it was reported that the Finns were the best miners in the community. In what had earlier been a wilderness, roads, churches, and settled communities appeared. By 1630 some thirty homesteads had been established. Two decades later the number had grown to one hundred and twenty, and at the close of the century, to about three hundred. According to Eli F. Heckscher, the number of farms in Värmland grew by more than 70 percent between 1560 and 1600, and in western Västmanland by more than 140 percent between 1630 and 1730.[10] These figures, which necessarily represent rough approximations because of the absence of adequate statistics, reflect pioneering on the frontier of older, settled parts of the kingdom that can be called "of very considerable dimensions." In this pioneering the settlers from Finland and their descendants played an important part.

Especially in a brief history like the present one, the frontier developments in central and western Sweden outlined above could well be reduced to the dimensions of a few sentences or a footnote, were it not for a fact that remains to be mentioned.

Between the years 1638 and 1655 (1655 marks

---

10. *Ibid.*, I, pp. 137, 23, 264, 401, 446.

the transfer of New Sweden to the Dutch) something like one-half the inhabitants on the Delaware were Finns. Most of them came, not directly from Finland, but from those provinces in Sweden that have been mentioned as the regions in which the Finns pioneered from the 1580's onward. While the Finns who came in search of fortune to the shores of the Delaware represented, as will be brought out later, only a fraction of those who had emigrated from Finland to Sweden, they became part of the New Sweden colonists, it appears, primarily because of the increasing restrictions placed upon them by the forest ordinances that have been mentioned. In a word, the Finnish frontiersmen in Sweden, having come into collision with public authority desirous of preserving the forest resources of the land and likewise with Swedes unwilling to lose old hunting, fishing, and other rights and opportunities, ultimately furnished a substantial number of the New Sweden colonists. It is this circumstance above others that relates the agricultural and other developments summarized in the preceding pages to the Finns on the Delaware.

Finally, the economic life of Sweden-Finland became more closely connected than earlier with the undertakings of foreign men of business. New resources in initiative and capital furnished by enterprising burghers from abroad provided much of the basis upon which the New Sweden venture in colonization rested.

In speaking of the period 1600-1720 the author of a work already frequently cited in these pages states that one of its outstanding characteristics was the circumstance that Sweden-Finland's economic life "came in a great many different ways under international influences greater than any in earlier days;" not until the nineteenth century, he suggests, did anything like correspondingly great influences from abroad make themselves felt in the kingdom.[11] Trade and commerce, the mining industries (whose importance was rapidly increasing), manufacturing, shipping, and shipbuilding—in short, nearly every phase of the economic life of the kingdom except agriculture—came to mean contributions and often control also by foreign merchants, manufacturers, and capitalists. More often than not they had emigrated to Sweden; with but few exceptions, they became subjects of the land of their adoption and, after a generation or two, fully acclimated in Sweden.

---

11. *Ibid.*, I, 23.

Among the men whose coming spelled new enterprises, new techniques in manufacturing and
mining, new forms of business and commercial organization, and new initiative in general, the Dutch,
the Germans, and the Scots were by far the most
important. The Dutch represented, almost literally,
a new element in Swedish economic development,
and the same may be said concerning the Scots.
The Germans stood in a category by themselves, for
Hanseatic and other commercial influences from
the Germanies were of old standing, going back to
the Middle Ages. But from 1600 on, the Dutch influence was the most significant and left the deepest
impression upon Sweden-Finland.[12]

That the Dutch, Scotch, and other foreign elements became important factors in Sweden-Finland,
especially during the first half of the seventeenth
century (Heckscher remarks, on page 364, with reference to this period, that "nearly all important undertakings in the field of economic enterprise came
from abroad or—usually—from foreigners"), was a
result of the liberal policy which the Crown formulated and followed. Loyalty toward King and Crown

---

12. The following paragraphs, summarizing some of the
main phases of these foreign influences, are largely based
upon *ibid.*, Vol. II, ch. iii.

and at least outward religious conformity appear to have been the most important conditions that the foreigner had to meet. Catholics and Jews, to be sure, were rigorously excluded. Language and place of origin were but secondary considerations. Subject to the conditions mentioned, the state accepted the foreigner and frequently hastened to give him an honored position in the country. One of the common favors bestowed by the Crown was elevation to the ranks of the nobility and the granting of lucrative positions in the service of the State; some 42 percent of all the families raised to noble rank in Sweden are, in fact, of foreign extraction.

A few illustrations of the treatment of the "new men" by the State will suffice to indicate the trend of the times. In the city of Gothenburg attempts were made to obtain Dutch burghers by making Dutch the sole official language of the city administration, and Gustavus Adolphus (1611-1632) granted permission to use Dutch equally with Swedish. In the first Gothenburg municipal government were found ten Dutchmen, one Scot, and seven Swedes; during the first thirty years of the history of this city, the *Burggreven* (the representative of the Crown in the city) was a Netherlander. Even such significant undertakings as the Copper Company (which was established under Gustavus Adolphus to handle the Crown monopoly in the manufacturing and sale of the most important export article of the period, namely, copper) had but one Swede among its directors after the issuance of its charter privileges of 1622.

The most striking example of the Dutch influence was perhaps Louis De Geer. A Walloon from the bishopric of Liége, who had been a merchant in Amsterdam and interested in the Swedish copper trade, he went to Sweden and became a Swedish subject in 1627. Ultimately he dominated the business enterprises of his day in a manner that makes it easier "to say what part of the economic life of Sweden he did not control, than to enumerate the phases dependent on his activity." He became the leading banker and creditor of the Crown and copper, grain, and salt merchant. He likewise became the greatest mine owner and the most conspicuous figure in the modernization of the iron industry. He owned establishments for the manufacture of arms, textiles, brass, and paper, and he owned shipyards and ships. He was interested in the founding of colonies in Africa, on the one hand, and in the running of retail business in a provincial Swedish city, on the other. While his extensive business enterprises were supervised by two offices located in Sweden, the center of his manifold undertakings appears to have been located in Amsterdam, Holland.

In Sweden's business and industrial life in his day, De Geer stands out like a giant among the foreigners of that period, not a few of whom were men of anything but small accomplishment. Taken together, they controlled many of the existing forms of economic activity and became the founders of new industries. Their influence, as has already been suggested, was great, and at many a point, decisive; the imprint they left upon their adopted country was far deeper and more lasting than their relatively small number would indicate.

Finally, the Dutch made a contribution to the development of the commercial company as an instrument of trade with the outside world. It was this phase of early seventeenth-century development in Sweden-Finland that may be said to constitute the immediate background of the founding of the New Sweden colony on the Delaware.

Commercial companies of the general type of the English East India Company and the Dutch East India Company—to mention only two of many—made their appearance in Sweden-Finland at a relatively early date. By the second decade of the seventeenth century they seem to have obtained a firm footing, and by the 1620's several commercial companies had been founded. In only two fields, however, did they become of lasting importance, namely, in the copper trade and in the export of naval stores, especially tar. But whether of temporary or of permanent importance, it was Dutch models and Dutch influence that accounted for the fact that Sweden-Finland embarked upon the then-modern way of mobilizing financial resources for purposes of foreign trade and also for the purpose of obtaining a share in the profits presumably offered by the founding of colonies across the seas.

II

THE RÔLE OF THE MERCHANTS

HISTORIANS frequently speak of the colonizing and commercial movements of the European world during the century following the discovery of America by Columbus as the "Commercial Revolution." By this term is meant the many-sided development by which European commercial interests and enterprises came to encompass ever larger parts of the world; exploration and colonization were a part of it, and an increase in the commercial and financial resources of the countries that were successful in their efforts to gain colonial empires was one of its consequences.

The seventeenth century was the period during which the new commercial opportunities opened up to Europeans by the discovery of the New World and the sea route to the East were increasingly captured by the nations of northern Europe. For instance, the Dutch, the English, and the French, having begun to challenge the Spaniard in North America even before the year 1600, succeeded in obtaining a foothold on this continent. Less than a third of a century later—by 1630—Virginia, the New England settlements, and New Amsterdam had been firmly established. Colonization under auspices other than Spanish had thus been begun in a manner that was destined to leave lasting impressions upon the future history of both the New World and the Old.

Perhaps the most common device or organization developed to exploit the growing trade and colonial opportunities of the period was the chartered commercial company. The rise of the commercial company was a general phenomenon over large parts of Europe: England, Holland, France, Denmark, Scotland, Prussia, and other countries chartered companies and encouraged their development. The London and Plymouth companies, which played a part in the establishment of the English possessions in America in the early seventeenth century, are familiar to all students of American colonial history. They were only two of a large number, however, the most famous of which was the English East India Company, organized in 1600. It was this company that carried on the conquest and also the government of India down to the year 1858.

Sweden-Finland was no exception as regards the utilization of this new departure in the conduct of mercantile activity. There also the individually owned or partnership business organization of earlier days was increasingly abandoned because of the advantages offered by the commercial company. A commercial company was chartered in Gothenburg in 1607 (the charter was issued, characteristically enough, in German) and a general trading company in 1615. Still another was launched in 1619 and given a monopoly of the foreign copper trade, which, as has already been suggested, was becoming important during these years. Several others are recorded during the decade of the 1620's, but most of them either barely got beyond the paper stage or failed without having made any permanent mark.[1] The same applies to many other enterprises that were launched between 1630 and about the middle of the century.

Among these early companies there were two that deserve more than passing mention, because they

---

1. These facts and those below pertaining to the commercial companies established before the appearance of the New Sweden Company in 1637 are taken in the main from Amandus Johnson's *The Swedish Settlements on the Delaware* (New York, 1911), chs. v-x.

furnish the background of the New Sweden Company, established in 1637.

The first was the South Company, established in December, 1624.[2] The man responsible for the South Company was a Netherlander, one of the many who had settled in Sweden, entered the service of the Swedish state, or become important figures in the lowlier but no less lucrative domain of commerce or industry. His name was Willem Usselinx. A founder of the Dutch West India Company, Usselinx had fallen out with his colleagues in the enterprise and left his native Holland in 1623. Journeying to Sweden, he was able in the fall of 1624 to present a scheme for the establishment of a trading company to Gustavus Adolphus. The proposal was favorably acted upon, and Usselinx was commissioned to found the South Company. The company's charter received the signature of the King in 1626.

The charter was to run for twelve years, and it provided that the company should carry on trade

---

2. The commission granted to its founder provided for the founding of a general trading company for "Asia, Africa, America and Magellanica." *Ibid.*, p. 53 n, mentions that the company was called by ten different names; the usual designation, however, was the South Company.

with the greater part of the non-European part of the world. The establishment of settlements in territories not occupied by other states was also contemplated, but this purpose represented, according to Amandus Johnson, only "a secondary object." As was customary in those days, monopoly rights were to be enjoyed by the company. The provisions for membership were liberal; foreigners were admitted and given special privileges. The headquarters were to be in Gothenburg. The Crown was to receive 20 percent of all minerals found and 10 percent of the produce of the lands cultivated under company auspices. Booty taken from pirates or enemies was to be used for the defense and protection of trade.

Despite the efforts made to find the necessary capital for the new company, its financing spelled difficulties from the start. To be sure, the King subscribed a large sum—450,000 *dalers*, or approximately $360,000—and by 1627 the list of subscribers was considerable. Some $20,000 was subscribed in Finland. It appears to have been easier to get subscriptions than money, however; even the pledge of the King, Usselinx discovered, could not be collected. Ultimately the directors of the company began to busy themselves with objectives that had little or nothing to do with the intended purposes of the venture. The exploitation of Russian trade, the building of ships for Spain, the Swedish salt trade, the establishment of a glass factory in Sweden, and manufacturing establishments such as ropewalks and linen mills and the like were planned by the directors. Some of them actually were carried beyond the planning stage.

The result of this unexpected turn of events was that Usselinx, who feared that the company would after all not develop into the kind of enterprise he had originally had in mind but would instead "dwindle down to a ropewalk and a shipyard," decided to leave Sweden. Having obtained his release from his commitments, he left Sweden in 1629. The South Company continued to exist; but shortly thereafter it was combined with another company.

The second was the Ship Company. In the very year of Usselinx's departure from Sweden the growing needs of Sweden-Finland for a greater merchant marine resulted in the formation of a Ship Company, the purpose of which was to bring forth greater financial resources for shipbuilding than either the merchants or the state treasury could furnish. The initiative was taken by the Crown; the founders of the Ship Company were the cities of the kingdom. The ships of the company "were to be used for commercial voyages, either by the cities themselves or by the Crown at a certain rate of freight money, as well as in the case of war for the aid and protection of the country against the enemy." [3]

Once again it was discovered that it was easier to establish a company than to find the capital necessary for its functioning. In order to overcome the difficulty of raising the funds needed, Gustavus Adolphus asked the two estates, the nobility and the clergy, to make contributions. The estates, after having considered the matter, proposed that the funds already collected for the South Company should be allocated to the needs of the Ship Company. The suggestion was accepted, and in the spring of 1630 the union of the two companies was authorized.

During the next half-dozen years the new company thus formed fitted out ships and carried on trade with various parts of Europe. It was destined to be of no greater permanent significance than its predecessors, however. The financing of the company involved a procedure which deserves mention, for it represented no isolated instance of fund rais-

---

3. *Ibid.*, p. 69.

ing. As Eli F. Heckscher has put it, "the Ship Company was almost a 'compulsory corporation,' in which failure to contribute meant attachment and sale of property; after it was combined with the South Company, subscribers who failed to make payment were on occasion put in jail." [4] That the authority of the State was used to force the hand of the subscribers discloses a situation which meant anything but the kind of trade conditions and opportunities that bring men of business voluntarily to risk investments in order to obtain returns.

Ultimately the objectives that Usselinx had had in mind led to more pretentious achievements than those mentioned above. That is to say, a successful commercial enterprise, including colonial objectives, was finally launched in 1637, and out of it came, in the year following, the New Sweden settlement on the Delaware.

The immediate background of this commercial enterprise was furnished by the oft-mentioned copper trade. By the 1630's, when Sweden-Finland had become involved in the costly wars on the Continent, the Crown had borrowed "millions with copper as security and many of its debts to Dutch mer-

---

4. *Op. cit.*, p. 598.

chants were paid by this metal, large quantities being always kept in the storehouses of Tripp and Company in Amsterdam." [5] The Crown was consequently affected by fluctuations in the price of copper and interested in keeping the price stable. New markets for copper became an important concern of the government. In 1628 the Swedish commissioner in Holland busied himself with proposals that concerned the copper trade to the West Indies, and four years later he called the attention of his government to a Hollander well acquainted with the West Indian trade, by the name of Samuel Blommaert. Blommaert became interested in the question of finding new markets for the all-important metal. By 1635 Chancellor Oxenstierna, among others, had come to look to the new world across the Atlantic as offering profitable markets for both Swedish copper and Swedish iron.

Into the plans which were thus being made for launching into transatlantic trade, the appearance of Peter Minuit on the scene introduced a new factor. Having been governor of New Amsterdam for several years, he had met difficulties in the discharge of his duties, was recalled by the Dutch West India

---

5. Johnson, op. cit., p. 87.

Company, and had returned to Holland in 1632. He offered his services to Blommaert, who had interests along the Delaware River, where he had purchased land in 1629. Blommaert reported the offer to Chancellor Oxenstierna, and ultimately, in 1636, Minuit offered his services to the Swedish Crown and presented "a project of New Sweden." The plan called for the occupation of land in North America and the establishment there of a colony to be called New Sweden.

By the fall of 1636 negotiations between the government on the one hand and the two Hollanders on the other had resulted in the appointment of Blommaert as the agent of the Swedish Crown. Minuit was asked to journey to Sweden, there to present a report. Not the least significant element in the formulation of the plans which clearly pointed to a colony across the seas was the contribution made during the negotiations by still another Hollander, Peter Spiring. The son of a wealthy Dutch merchant, he engaged in business in Sweden and was a participant in the new project from the start. Spiring was later knighted in Sweden, and he became the founder of the Silfvercrona family.

Finally, in 1637, the New Sweden Company came into existence. It was organized by authority of Axel Oxenstierna, the Chancellor and member of the regency during Queen Christina's minority. Making full allowance for the contributions made to the establishment of the company by Blommaert, Minuit, and Spiring, "the most important promoter of this Company was Klas Fleming, an admiral in the Swedish navy." [6]

Klas Fleming was born in Louhisaari, in Finland, in 1592. The son of one of the leading Finnish nobles, who was a provincial governor, Klas Fleming received the education and training customary among the Finnish and Swedish aristocracy of that day. He took a degree at Wittenberg in 1609 and studied for a time at other German universities as well. At the age of twenty he returned from abroad. Shortly thereafter he took service in the regiment of his fellow countryman and relative Marshall Evert Horn, another representative of the higher Finnish

---

6. George H. Ryden, *The Story of New Sweden*, p. 3. Reprinted from the *American-Scandinavian Review*. Amandus Johnson, in speaking of the negotiations resulting in the New Sweden Company, says with reference to the closing weeks of the year 1636 that "Fleming was appointed to correspond with Spiring about it and the affair entered a new stage, Fleming's connection with the undertaking becoming of great importance for its future success." *Op. cit.*, p. 101.

aristocracy. In 1614 Gustavus Adolphus appointed him chamberlain, and during the years following he rose rapidly. In 1620 he was appointed vice-admiral of the fleet, and in 1629 he became the chief of the naval forces of the kingdom.

Under Fleming's leadership the navy was greatly increased and rendered more effective as a part of the ever-growing fighting forces of Sweden-Finland. But his services in other fields were no less important. In 1625 he became royal councillor, and after the death of Gustavus Adolphus seven years later, he was appointed a member of the regency. In 1637 when the College of Commerce—Board of Trade—was established, he became its president. The South Company and the enterprises which, as has been noted, led to the establishment of the New Sweden Company, were supported by him, financially and otherwise. It appears to be no exaggeration to say that, especially after he was appointed director of the New Sweden Company, Fleming became the leading spirit of the work which brought New Sweden into being as an accomplished fact in 1638.

Three Dutchmen (Blommaert, Spiring, and Minuit), a Swede (Chancellor Oxenstierna), and a Finn (Klas Fleming) thus played decisive parts in the formation of the New Sweden Company. Of the five, Fleming became the most important directive force during the early formative years of the settlements across the seas.

It may be said that the commercial companies of the 1600's were of two types. The first type was illustrated by the English and the Dutch companies, which came into being through the initiative of merchants desirous of exploiting trading opportunities at home and abroad on a large scale. The second type owed its existence not primarily to the enterprise of men of business but to that of the state; merchants did not necessarily welcome the latter, were none too quick to take part in their financing, and on occasion were definitely opposed to them.[7] Companies in this second group reflected political, territorial, and other objectives of the state rather than trade expansion resulting from a natural need for markets and new techniques of exchange. While the distinction between the two was not as sharp as this statement might suggest—for companies in the first group frequently enjoyed special favors of various kinds granted by the Crown—it is useful to keep it in mind in appraising especially the Swedish company making summarized in the preceding pages.

---

7. Cf. Heckscher, op. cit., p. 597.

From what has been noted it is clear that the companies discussed belonged to the latter group. This is indicated by the manner in which the necessary capital was obtained, or, more accurately, by the efforts made to get capital. Pressure was exerted by the Crown, and, as has been suggested, mere persuasion was not always sufficient to turn subscriptions into actual cash.

In several ways the New Sweden Company represented a new departure. The charter of the company having been lost, we do not know in complete detail the provisions under which the company was to carry on. But we do know that no definite capital stock was agreed upon. The cost of the first contemplated expedition to the New World was estimated, and each member agreed to furnish a part of the cost. There were but eleven members in the company; six of them were Dutch, if we classify Peter Spiring as a Swede, as Amandus Johnson does.[8] The Dutch members contributed one-half of the estimated cost of 36,000 florins (approximately $18,000). Blommaert alone paid one-half of the Dutch contribution. The share of Klas Fleming, the

---

8. *Op. cit.*, p. 106. The figures that follow are taken from the same work, pp. 106-119.

director, was one-sixteenth of the total amount.

The entrance of Sweden-Finland into the field of commercial and colonial enterprise overseas was thus made under the auspices of a company that was financed by only a handful of men and in which the Dutch element was significant, to say the least. Furthermore, Peter Minuit was appointed leader of the first expedition. A large part of the cargo and apparently half the crew of the two ships that constituted the first expedition likewise came from Holland, and Hendrick Huygen, a relative of Peter Minuit, was designated as the commissioner of the colony that was to be established. Of the twenty-three soldiers that were sent with the ships, some hailed from Holland.[9]

The organization of the New Sweden Company was completed by the early part of 1637, but several months elapsed before the first expedition was ready for the voyage to America. At long last two ships, *Kalmar Nyckel* and *Fogel Grip*, were acquired for the expedition, the cargo was obtained and crew

---

9. See Christopher Ward, *New Sweden on the Delaware* (Philadelphia, 1938), pp. 34-35; Amandus Johnson, *op. cit.*, p. 112. How many of the soldiers were Swedes, and whether they included men from the Finnish part of the kingdom, is apparently unknown.

hired, and other necessary preparations were completed. The ships left Sweden probably in the early part of November, 1637. After a stormy month of sailing they arrived on the island of Texel, in Holland, underwent repairs, restocked with provisions, and at the close of December set sail for the distant coast of North America.

The details of the long journey across the Atlantic are unknown. About the middle of March, 1638, the ships reached the Delaware River.

III

THE NEWCOMERS, 1638-1664

THE territory on which Peter Minuit landed and which he shortly thereafter purchased from the Indians did not represent regions previously unknown to Europeans or unclaimed by them. Nor did the small band of Minuit's followers represent the first settlers on the Delaware.

Leaving out of consideration several earlier explorers and mariners who may have visited the river, it is known that Henry Hudson, the Englishman who had entered the service of the Dutch East India Company, anchored in the Delaware Bay in 1609. A Dutch interest in the territory was thus established. In 1610 the English appeared on the scene. In 1616 a Dutch expedition came to the river, and shortly thereafter (1620) Cornelis May, of Hoorn, sailed up the Delaware, which the Dutch had come to call the South River. By 1623, two years after the founding of the Dutch West India Company, a trading post and a fortress (Fort Nassau) had been established, although it was abandoned a few years later and temporarily reoccupied in 1633. But by 1638, when Minuit arrived, Fort Nassau had been rebuilt and was garrisoned by the Dutch. In 1631 a Dutch colony was begun at Swaanendael, present-day Lewes, Delaware. This colony also was short-lived.

In the meantime the English colony to the south, in Virginia, had taken firm root. In 1632 the land grant made by Charles I to Lord Baltimore included territory partly carved out of the grant originally made to the Virginia Company, and a section of the Delaware River region. Thus both the Dutch and the English considered themselves to have prior and superior claims to the territory, and neither renounced their claims during the seventeen years that the Swedish flag flew over the New Sweden settlements.[1]

---

1. Johnson says, in speaking of the claim that Charles I transferred English rights to the Delaware territory to Sweden sometime between 1630 and 1634, that he is "strongly inclined to believe that some document from King Charles existed (dating from this time or earlier), either granting Swedish vessels the right to visit English colonies in America, or giving privileges to Sweden to erect trading posts on unoccupied territory, or both. . . ." *Op. cit.*, p. 178. No evidence beyond the assumption that the claim could hardly be mere invention is presented, however.

The landing of the expedition headed by Minuit is frequently spoken of as the establishment of a new colony in America. Actually, however, the so-called first colony was not a colony at all. It was only a trading post.[2] Neither the *Kalmar Nyckel* nor the *Fogel Grip* brought any settlers, as we have seen. Real colonists, farmers and mechanics, in considerable numbers and with families, desirous of establishing permanent homes, would be needed before New Sweden would develop into a colony worthy of the name. Of persons in this category the two ships carried none; excepting the crews, their human cargo consisted of some twenty-odd soldiers, a commissary, a commandant, and Minuit himself. It was only considerably later that real colonists arrived.

Carrying out the instructions he had received, Minuit proceeded to make arrangements for a permanent post on the river. Sailing up the Christina Creek, he established contact with Indians, and by the end of March he had purchased land from them, making payment in merchandise. The contracts recording the purchase have been lost, but the land

---

2. This observation, which in my opinion is in keeping with the facts, is made by Christopher Ward, *op. cit.*, p. 35.

transferred to the New Sweden Company appears to have extended, according to the Swedish claim, some forty miles along the Delaware below Christina Creek and about twenty-seven miles north, as far as the Schuylkill River. All the land purchased lay to the west of the river, the eastern bank not having been included. No western boundary was mentioned. Later purchases extended New Sweden to the falls of Trenton, and included territory on the eastern shore of the river as well. After the completion of the purchase, formal possession of the land in the name of Sweden took place. The construction of a fort was begun about two miles from the Delaware on the Christina Creek. Trade with Indians was also started, but with only moderate results. The Delaware was reconnoitred as far as and beyond Fort Nassau, which was located on the east bank of the river, roughly due south from present-day Philadelphia. The Dutch challenged Minuit's right to locate on the river, but it appears that they did not consider themselves strong enough to use force against the newcomers. When the work on the fort (which, by the way, could not command the Delaware, being two miles from it, on the bank of one of its tributaries) had gotten well under way and other arrangements had been made for the security of its small garrison, Minuit lifted anchor on the *Kalmar Nyckel* about the middle of June, after a stay of more than three months. The sister ship, the *Fogel Grip*, had been sent to cruise in the West Indian waters, with a view to profitable piracy at the expense of the Spaniards; it did not return to the Delaware until early in 1639 and therefore did not accompany the *Kalmar Nyckel* on its return voyage.

Peter Minuit was drowned at St. Kitts in the West Indies, and thus ended his connection with New Sweden. After the two ships had at long last returned to Sweden and the furs and other incidental cargo brought by them had been disposed of, the promoters of the enterprise discovered that the first expedition showed a heavy loss. Contrary to original calculations calling for expenditures of about $18,000, the expenses had risen to some $23,000. The furs and other return cargo brought less than $10,000. On the credit side of the ledger could be placed, of course, the fort on Christina Creek, manned by twenty-odd men waiting for the next expedition bringing merchandize necessary for the trade with the Indians, needed tools and implements, and above all, settlers, without which a mere trading post could not develop into a colony.

In view of what will be said in this chapter regarding the Finnish element among the Delaware pioneers, one or two observations should be made at the outset. First, no attempt has been made to break the facts pertaining to the Finns out of their natural context for the purpose of giving extra emphasis to them among the settlers, at the expense of the Swedes. In the summaries of the expeditions which were undertaken between 1638 and 1655, the pertinent facts relating to emigrants are given. A substantial part of the detailed material presented by Johnson [3] deals with the Finns. In other words, the vast amount of information collected by Johnson, in so far as it enables us to distinguish be-

---

3. Johnson's chapters on the expeditions (xv, xviii, xxv-xxix, xxxix, xl, xlix, liv), upon which this account is based, are so detailed as to justify the statement that the author presents what in a sense amounts to a collection of the material available on the subject. This fortunate circumstance makes it possible even for one who has not had the opportunity to study the original sources to obtain a view of the problem which no ordinary secondary work could give. There seems good reason to believe that Johnson's meticulous collection of materials has been carried to such a point that whenever his treatment of a given expedition is scanty, the explanation in all likelihood is lack of information, not the author's failure to push the inquiry to its utmost limits.

tween the two groups among the pioneers on the Delaware, is such as to emphasize time and again the Finnish element in the settlements. It leads to the conclusion that a large part of the population was Finnish. No forced interpretation of the information available underlies the conclusions formulated.

Secondly, the question of how many of the New Sweden settlers were Finns and how many should be classified as Swedes cannot be easily answered by references to their names alone. The names of both Finns and Swedes were nearly always given —especially in public records and the like—in Swedish. This is clearly shown, for instance, by the following names, which are mentioned as belonging to Finnish settlers in the colony: Eskil Larsson, Klement Jöransson, Jöns Påfvelsson, Bertel Eskelsson, Clemet, Anders, Johan, Måns, Clemet Mickelsson, Hendrick, Karin, Lasse, Evert Hindricksson, Måns Jurrensson, Hinrick Matzon, Matts Hansson, Knut Martensson, Karl Jansson, Johan Fransson. Because it is thus impossible to distinguish between Finns and Swedes by referring to names, no attempt has been made to indulge in fanciful interpretation of names. Anyone familiar with the history of Finland and the Finns realizes that nothing is more misleading—especially down to a generation or two ago—than the attempt to determine nationality on the basis of an analysis of family names without detailed genealogical information. The narrative in these pages avoids this phase of the matter.

If, then, what is ordinarily assumed to have been only a minor element in the population of New Sweden is given more substantial proportions as the narrative proceeds, the result flows from the facts presented by the author of the only large-scale treatment of the history of New Sweden.

As one surveys the eleven expeditions made to New Sweden after Minuit had nominally established the settlement, the main impressions gathered from the evidence that has come down to us are of frustration and failure. During the years 1638-1644 Klas Fleming, the moving spirit of the New Sweden Company, attempted time and again to augment the human and other resources of the settlers, but his efforts met with only moderate success. Lack of capital seems to have hampered the company from the very start, and this handicap remained an ever-present obstacle during the seventeen years that the Delaware region flew the Swedish flag. The ships used by the company appear to have been poor, crews were hard to get, and necessary merchandize was obtained only with difficulty. Except during the closing years of the period 1638-1655, the problem of finding colonists appears to have defied solution, and at no time were the leaders of the New Sweden Company successful in providing the colony with adequate military or naval support.

The story of the actual settlement of New Sweden is therefore the story of expeditions inadequately prepared, in many instances interminably delayed, not only by the hazards of navigation, but also by the inadequacy of human and material resources. The ultimate result was that the number of Swedes and Finns on the Delaware never exceeded a few hundred souls. For a considerable part of the seventeen-year period there were only a few scores, largely soldiers, carrying on the tasks necessary for keeping alive in a pioneer settlement, while constantly waiting for aid from far-away Sweden-Finland.

The second expedition was delayed for more than two years. It was not until April, 1640, that the next ship arrived. Klas Fleming had been busy preparing a second expedition since the summer of 1638. It was his intention to send a large expedition, and strenuous efforts appear to have been made to secure real colonists. It will be recalled that Peter Minuit had brought no settlers in 1638 and that the twenty-odd men he left at Fort Christina were all soldiers, one-half of whom were Dutch. Fleming attempted to lay the foundation of a real settlement by sending farmers and artisans whose coming would change a mere trading post, precariously held, into a colony solidly planted in the more substantial life and work of farmer-colonists.

The attempt to obtain bona fide colonists was not successful, however, and recourse was had to a policy which became, one might say, the rule rather than the exception for several years to come. That is, provincial governors and others were instructed to apprehend lawbreakers of various kinds—poachers, persons guilty of breaking forest ordinances, deserted soldiers, debtors unable to pay, and others who had run afoul of the law—and to send them and their families to the Delaware. Johnson surmises that the governors "were undoubtedly successful in the efforts" to round up emigrants of this type, but concludes that "we do not know to what extent, as the exact number of colonists sent over on this expedition cannot be ascertained." [4]

It is worthy of note, however, that two of the three provinces included in this forcible recruiting of settlers were Värmland and Dalsland, both of

---

4. Johnson, op. cit., pp. 127-128.

which had received a substantial addition to their
population by the emigration of Finns, noted in the
first chapter, since about 1580. In both, the Finnish
frontier pioneers had come to feel, by the end of
the 1630's, the pressure of the new policy of the
Crown regarding the use of forests, and, as was observed, the ordinances against the wasteful use of
forests were primarily directed against them. These
circumstances do not constitute anything like definite proof of the presence of Finns among the emigrants, but in the absence of other evidence, they
seem to justify the presumption that Finns were
among the first real settlers that came to the Delaware in 1640. Incidentally, not one of the ten
colonists known to have arrived on the second expedition is definitely identified as to the locality in
Sweden-Finland from which he came.[5]

When the ship that arrived in April, 1640, sailed
for Sweden, "several people" returned with the
ship. It therefore appears that after their departure,
the unpretentious settlement remained, as far as

5. *Ibid.*, p. 710. Professor Nils Ahnlund, one of the leading Swedish historians, concludes that "the first real emi-
grant to New Sweden, Peter Gunnarsson Rambo, and his
wife Brita Mattsdotter," came from Vaasa, Finland. *Ymer*,
1937, No. 4, p. 268.

numbers are concerned, virtually unchanged, and still constituted a colony in name only.

It had been Minuit's intention to bring colonists from Holland to New Sweden. His death on the return voyage from America brought the plan to an end, but before long a movement was afoot in Holland, the purpose of which was to obtain permission from Sweden to settle on the Delaware. Klas Fleming was interested in the project, but the Royal Council postponed action until January, 1640, when a charter was issued allowing settlers from Holland to establish a colony some twenty miles north of Fort Christina. Obstacles to the scheme appeared, however, both the Dutch States General and the Dutch West India Company being opposed to it, and it was not until November, 1640, that the Hollanders arrived in America. It appears that it had been contemplated to send some fifty colonists, but the number of those who came is unknown; Johnson's sources furnish no information on this point.

Immediately after the return of the first expedition in 1639, the Dutch members of the New Sweden Company desired to withdraw from the undertaking, but funds necessary to buy them out could not be found. In the following year an agreement eliminating the Dutch from participation in the company was made, and in January, 1641, their connection with the company was severed, funds to pay them having been obtained. The company thus became free from foreign influences. Klas Fleming, who had been its director from the first, retained his post in the reorganized company and continued to manage its affairs as before.

It is interesting to note that the elimination of Dutch participation coincided with the first appearance of real colonists in the New Sweden enterprise of which we have definite record. Preparations for a fourth voyage to America began in 1640. After delays of various kinds extending over a year, two ships left for the Delaware in August, 1641. They arrived at their destination in November of the same year.

In the recruiting of colonists for this expedition the difficulty of obtaining voluntary emigrants led again to the use of the procedure noted in connection with the voyage in 1640. That is to say, force was employed. One of the provincial governors was instructed to "endeavor to entice people together, with wives and children, cattle and horses and all goods," [6] and to persuade them to go to New

---

6. Johnson (*op. cit.*, p. 146) translates the original "sammanlocka folk" as "collect people," but I believe "entice people" to be more correct and to reflect more accurately the nature of the effort.

Sweden. Furthermore, efforts were made to reach the Finns in central and western Sweden, with a view to obtaining colonists from the frontier settlements established by them. Especially those among the Finns who had collided with the law were considered potential emigrants. Recruiting by sending out agents was tried, and some colonists were obtained through their efforts.

But sterner methods were also used. Thus, a provincial governor was instructed by the Royal Council in February, 1641, that, other efforts failing, he should apprehend the Finns in his district guilty of destroying forests and hold them ready to be shipped to America on the ship that was being made ready for the voyage. Johan Printz, who became governor of New Sweden in 1643, was stationed in Finland at the time and received instructions to recruit emigrants in Finland. Still another provincial governor in Sweden proper, who "had captured a number of the Finns and kept them in prison awaiting the orders of the Government," was directed to permit "all the Finns whom he had captured, who could not give bonds, to leave for the colony. . . . If they refused to go they should be punished." [7]

---

7. Quotations from Johnson, op. cit., pp. 150-151.

The expedition consisted of two ships, which arrived on the Delaware in November, 1641. The number of colonists is but partly recorded, no list of the majority of the emigrants having been preserved. The partial list, containing thirty-five names, is published in full in Johnson, pages 151-153. Thirteen of the persons listed are recorded in a manner that permits reasonable conclusions as to the locality from which they hailed. Two of them are listed as "Finns," two are listed as coming from Finland, nine from Sweden proper. Whether these nine included Finns cannot be determined.

However small the expedition of 1641 was, it appears to have led to the establishment of two settlements beyond Fort Christina. One of them was Finland, located between present-day Marcus Hook and Chester (and partly including land now within the limits of Chester), Pennsylvania. The other was Uppland, approximately where Chester is now located. These were the first permanent settlements in territory that later became the state of Pennsylvania.

Some fifteen months elapsed before the next ships came from Sweden. Whether the expedition that arrived in February, 1643, brought any considerable number of colonists is not known. Efforts had been made to secure colonists, to be sure. Requests for more people having been received from New Sweden, the Royal Council again sent out letters to provincial governors urging them to prevail upon people to leave for America. Omitting some of the detail of these efforts—the detail relates to a few persons who were obtained in Finland—the substance of these efforts may be put as follows.

But few emigrants were willing to go, and more effective means than mere persuasion had to be employed. In the summer [of 1642] the council decided that poachers and deserted soldiers should be condemned to serve in the colony for a number of years. But even in this way the number found was insufficient, and in August several governors of the northern and central provinces of the kingdom were requested to capture such Finns in their territories as were known to be destroying the forests and doing damage to the woods at the mines. These people with their families were to be kept in readiness for transportation to Gothenburg. . . . Later it was decided that citizens also who could not pay their debts should be deported.[8]

Of the twenty-two persons recorded as having arrived in New Sweden in 1643, seventeen were listed as soldiers.[9]

8. *Ibid.*, p. 239.
9. *Ibid.*, pp. 714-715.

It seems correct to say, in the light of these facts, that in so far as this expedition, nearly five years after Peter Minuit arrived with his small band of soldiers, increased the number of settlers on the Delaware, the addition in all likelihood represented a Finnish element. It should also be noted that when the two ships returned to Sweden, three colonists mentioned by name "and many others returned with the vessels," and that it would therefore in all likelihood be misleading to speak of any substantial growth of the settlements at this time.

The same applies to the ship *Fama*, which arrived in March, 1644. Klas Fleming had once more contributed his untiring activity on behalf of the colony, but the results of his labors were again anything but impressive. As had been the case on several earlier occasions, merchandize and other commodities appear to have been a more important part of the ship's cargo than settlers. Speaking of the latter, Johnson remarks that "it appears that two or three colonists came from Finland," and states that besides "these I have found no traces of emigrants, who came here on this expedition." [10]

If the expedition of the year 1644 was of no im-

10. *Ibid.*, p. 243.

portance in the growth of New Sweden, another event which occurred in the same year appears to have had a marked effect upon its development. A war between Sweden and Denmark broke out, and in one of the naval engagements Klas Fleming, the admiral of the Swedish fleet, was killed. In him "the company and the colony lost their best friend and most enthusiastic promoter." Chancellor Oxenstierna now became the unappointed director of the company, but he lacked time—and perhaps inclination also—to superintend its activities. For several years the settlements on the Delaware were left to shift for themselves even more than they had been under Fleming's directorship.

Two expeditions were sent between 1644 and 1648. Only a few colonists came during these years. The information which has been preserved concerning the cargoes suggests that we are still dealing with trading posts rather than with a colony, although settled communities had come into being by the close of the first decade of the history of New Sweden. In 1648 New Sweden consisted of six fortified places, from Fort Christina in the south to Fort New Korsholm, on the Schuylkill, to the north; one, Fort Elfsborg, was on the eastern shore of the Delaware, in present-day New Jersey.

The population of New Sweden at that time was small. The total number of male inhabitants in 1648 was eighty-three. In 1644 it had been 105. In 1647 the population had amounted to 183 souls; the number of freemen settled on farms in that year was 28. Dissatisfaction with conditions and the consequent tendency to leave the Delaware, sickness, and other factors decimated the small population, and, as has been noted, ships returning to Sweden frequently carried persons anxious to return to their homeland. The settlements thus faced the second decade of the Swedish experiment in colony building with prospects that were anything but promising.

Despite the fact that since the death of Klas Fleming in 1644 there had been no director able to devote his time to the business of managing the company, a change in the growth of the Delaware settlements took place during the last seven years of Swedish rule. That is to say, for some years after 1648 the number of emigrants leaving Sweden-Finland grew considerably. Also, the governorship of Johan Printz—he was appointed in 1643 and served until 1653—appears to have spelled more energetic leadership of the affairs of the settlements in America. Printz proceeded to perfect the Swedish control of the river and of the trade with the Indians. The first fort on the eastern, or New Jersey, shore was constructed and named Fort Elfsborg; the administrative center was moved from Fort Christina to Tinicum Island, at present Essington, in the state of Pennsylvania, some twelve miles south of Philadelphia. In general, his activities had the effect of adding to the settled area of New Sweden and of pushing its limits further northward.

But the economic aspect of the colony left much to be desired. Printz reported to his superiors that crops were poor and the fur trade bad and that oxen and food had to be purchased from the Dutch at New Amsterdam. Sickness was prevalent among the small population, which numbered some one hundred souls when Printz arrived. Twenty persons died in the fall of 1643, the year when Printz began to stimulate the few ailing settlements then in existence into more robust life. During the next half-dozen years the colony was barely able to hold its own with regard to numbers.

Even after 1648 an increase in the number of people in Sweden-Finland willing to emigrate to the Delaware Valley did not mean that the colony grew rapidly. The expedition sent in 1649 promised at first a substantial increase in the number of settlers.

In the record of the preparations for the voyage we once again find Finns prominently mentioned. Indeed, as on several earlier occasions, nearly all of the detailed information deals with them. Some two hundred Finns, it was reported to the authorities, wished to go to New Sweden, and in the minutes of the Royal Council under the date of July 12, 1649, it was stated that "300 (?) Finns" requested permission to leave for the Delaware. Whether permission was given is not known, nor is it possible to tell how many of the seventy persons who actually left for America were Finns and how many were Swedes. The ship carrying the settlers ran aground in the West Indies, and never reached its destination. The greater part of its passengers and crew died on the way. Some twenty would-be settlers ultimately returned to their native land to tell of the tragedy which had befallen their expedition.

Before the disastrous voyage of 1649, expeditions had been fairly frequent, although the number of settlers had been small. Between 1649 and 1655, when the Dutch finally asserted their claim to the Delaware Valley by seizing it and thus bringing the sovereignty of Sweden to an end, only one expedition arrived. A second was sent, to be sure, but instead of reaching the Delaware, it sailed by mistake to New Amsterdam and was prevented from continuing to its destination.

The first of these arrived in May, 1654. It grew out of preparations similar to those noted in connection with most earlier expeditions. Recourse was had to recruiting, especially in the provinces of Värmland and Dalsland, and in view of what is known of the Finnish element in the earlier collection of emigrants from these provinces, the likelihood that they again furnished a part of the recruits is considerable. The exact number of newcomers is unknown, however, for the roll list has not been preserved. Johnson says that "a great many colonists went over with the expedition, but we are unable to state the exact number or their names for the roll-list has been lost." [11] Many died during the voyage, which appears to have been exceptionally hard.

Not long before the arrival of the settlers in America, Governor Johan Printz had rounded out a service of ten years on the Delaware. During the decade he had stood at the head of the small band of Swedes and Finns who constituted the subjects of his domain, Printz had dispatched lengthy reports

11. *Ibid.,* pp. 482, 471-472.

and descriptions of the settlements, and had urged the necessity of sending more colonists, better equipment—both military and other—and more merchandize, without which the trade with the Indians could not well be carried on. The response to his recommendations and pleas was silence or aid in men and supplies that fell far short of meeting the needs of the struggling settlements. On the whole, these years were marked by a governmental policy of neglect which could not but stifle the development of the enterprise which Printz headed.

In April, 1653—about a year before the arrival of the tenth expedition—Printz described the population of New Sweden in the following words:

The people yet living and remaining in New Sweden, men, women, and children, number altogether two hundred souls. The settled families do well, and are supplied with cattle. The country yields a fair revenue. Still the soldiers and others in the Company's service enjoy but a very mean subsistence, and consequently seek opportunity every day to get away, whether with or without leave, having no expectation of any release, as it is now five and a half years since a letter was received from home. The English trade, from which we used to obtain good support, is at an end, on account of the war with Holland; while the fur trade yields no profit, particularly now that hostilities have broken out between the Arrihoga and the Susquehanna Indians, from whom the beavers were procured.[12]

Probably discouraged by the failure to obtain adequate support from home, Printz returned to Sweden in the same year, never to return. The settlers on the Delaware were thus deprived of leadership which, while it appears to have been harsh and even cruel—Printz was a man of anything but mild and humane temperament—had been in marked contrast to the leadership in New Sweden before Printz came to these shores. The last two years of Swedish dominion on the Delaware were to show that Sweden-Finland was unable to provide another leader capable of sustaining the effort which Minuit had begun and Printz energetically continued.

By the time the next expedition arrived in New Sweden, in the early part of 1656, the flag of Sweden had ceased to fly on the Delaware. It had been replaced by that of the Dutch. We therefore turn to note the situation which ended the short chapter of Sweden-Finland's experiment in colony building in the New World.

---

12. Quoted in Justin Winsor, *Narrative and Critical History of America* (1889), IV, 469-470.

E-N-N- NIEW JO

NIEW J Wappinges

t'Schepinaikonck

Meoech konck Waranawankon Waor

Mecharienkonck Tams Kami Wappinges Kill

Kaes Eylant

t'Schichte Wacki Harretschoen Pacham

Wischers Rack Nanichi Sr

COLONIE Clicker Betuc

VAN Bergh Verdrietige

Schoon greyne Tappaans Nieu Amsterda manhattans

Bosch DE HEER NEDER

Pechqua kock HORST Xevers

milfort Nieuw Amsterda

Minquaas. Bergen River Breuckelen Jamaica

R S Lacus achter Col Parvus amersfort

Sanhicans greenwych

Cahoos oft Waterval Rariton Rechkt

Sanhicans Engelsche Plan

Mageckqueshou Vere Souts

Verbulsten Eylant Matovancons Groote Riv

Sauwan Quakers hoeck

oos Aquauachu ques

Ermomex Rootenberghs hoeck

Fort Nassou Amacaronck Barndegat

Naratickback Arme Vemer

Verckers kill Moetcon Karonck Everhaven

Fort Elsenburgh Barndegat

Naraticons

Swanendael Nieuw

Hoere Kill port May

Carp May

C. Cornelius

REPRODUCTION of a part of the Nicholas
Visscher Map, published in 1655 and re-
vised in 1683. Courtesy of New York
Public Library

It was observed at the beginning of this chapter that several years before the arrival of the Swedes and the Finns on the Delaware, the Dutch had appeared in that region. A trading post and a fortress at Fort Nassau had been built in 1623, and other places on the river had been temporarily occupied by them. At no time between 1638 and 1655 did the Dutch recede from the position they had assumed as soon as Peter Minuit and his followers arrived, namely, that their claim to the territory was superior to that of any other nation. This was clearly brought out in a communication which William Kieft, governor of the New Netherlands, sent to Minuit under the date May 8, 1638.

I . . . make known to you, Peter Menuet, who style yourself Commander in the service of Her Royal Majesty, the Queen of Sweden [wrote Kieft] that the whole South River of the New Netherlands . . . has already, for many years, been our property, occupied by our forts, and sealed with our blood; which was also done when you were a servant in the New Netherlands, and you are, therefore, well aware of this. But whereas you have now come between our forts to build a fortress to our injury and prejudice, which we shall never permit; as we are also assured that Her Royal Majesty of Sweden has never given you authority to build forts upon our rivers and coasts, nor to settle people on the land, nor to traffic in peltries, nor to undertake anything to our injury: We do, therefore protest against all the injury to property, and all the evil consequences of bloodshed, uproar, and wrong which our Trading Company may thus suffer: And that we shall protect our rights in such manner as we may find most advisable.[13]

Minuit paid no heed to the warning, and seventeen years were to elapse before the Dutch protest stiffened into definite action, resulting in the expulsion of Sweden from North America.

The Dutch threat to New Sweden was fully understood. Thus Governor Printz wrote to Stockholm in 1647:

It is of the utmost necessity for us to see how we can get rid of the Dutch from the river, for they oppose us on every side: (1) They destroy our trade everywhere. (2) They strengthen the savages with guns, shot, and powder, publicly trading with these against the edict of all Christians. (3) They stir up the savages to attack us, which, but for our prudence, would already have happened. (4) They begin to buy land from the savages within our boundaries, which we had purchased already eight years ago, and have the im-

---

13. A. C. Myers (ed.), *Narratives of Early Pennsylvania, West New Jersey and Delaware, 1630-1707* (New York, 1912), p. 63.

pudence here and there to erect the seal of the West India Company, calling it their arms; moreover, they give New Sweden the name of New Netherland, and are not ashamed to build their houses there.[14]

The lack of man power prevented any real attempt to challenge the Dutch, and they remained a threat throughout the Swedish period.

Leaving out of consideration some earlier minor clashes, the Dutch began seriously to assert their authority in 1651. In May of that year a Dutch ship was anchored in the Delaware, a few miles below Fort Christina, for the purpose of closing the river. This measure was not long-lived, however, but more serious was the establishment shortly thereafter of Fort Casimir. Fort Casimir was built some five miles below Fort Christina (present-day New Castle), on the western shore of the river. When completed, it could effectively block the river and cut off the Swedes and Finns to the north from direct contact by water with the outside world. Land purchases from the Indians were also made, and conflicting claims to land already bought by Minuit and his followers presented. By 1653 more than a score of Dutch families had settled around the new fort.

The delicate situation created by these develop-

_____
14. *Ibid.*, p. 123.

ments was completely changed in 1654. In a memorial which the Swedish government issued for the guidance of Printz and Johan Rising, Printz's successor, instructions had been given to secure both sides of the river, but the use of force had not been contemplated. The instructions relating to Fort Casimir stated:

If the Dutch could not be removed by argument and grave remonstrances and everything else which can be done without danger and hostility, then . . . [it would be] better *in terminis protestandi* to tolerate the Dutch there, than that the same fort should fall into the hands of the English.[15]

The erection of a Swedish fort below Fort Casimir was advised, in order to secure the control of the river, but an attack upon the Dutch was considered "incompatible with the weak power of the Swedes."

Johan Rising accompanied the expedition which arrived in May, 1654. Upon reaching the river, his first important action was to disregard his instructions and to capture Fort Casimir. The capture was easily effected, for the garrison was small and lacked gunpowder. The twenty-odd Dutch families

---

15. Quoted in Johnson, *op. cit.*, p. 581. Johnson tells the story of the overthrow of New Sweden by the Dutch in ch. xlvii.

that had settled at Fort Casimir were forced to swear allegiance to their new sovereign. Thus the Swedes and the Finns could say that at long last the Delaware had been freed from all foreign control.

The sequel to the seizure of the fort was not long in coming. Governor Peter Stuyvesant received word of Rising's action about a week after the surrender of the fort and reported the matter to the Dutch West India Company in Holland. Part of the score was evened by Stuyvesant in September of the same year, when a ship carrying a handful of colonists from Sweden to the Delaware settlements sailed to New Amsterdam by mistake and was captured by the Dutch. In Holland the news of Rising's procedure led to preparations for strengthening Stuyvesant's hand and to the decision that the entire Delaware Valley should be captured. By November, 1654, preparations for a punitive expedition were under way, and Stuyvesant was instructed to "do his utmost to revenge this misfortune not only by restoring matters to their former condition, but also by driving the Swedes at the same time from the river." [16]

16. Quoted in *ibid.*, p. 591.

To make a long story short, after several delays Stuyvesant appeared on the river, in the closing days of August, 1655, accompanied by a force variously estimated at from 300 to 700 men. Fort Casimir—which had been renamed Fort Trefaldighet by Rising—was taken on September 1. Two weeks later Fort Christina likewise fell into the hands of the Dutch. No real resistance to the Dutch was offered, and the Dutch flag supplanted the Swedish with almost no bloodshed. As subsequent events were to show, the Swedes and Finns on the Delaware would henceforth pioneer first under the Dutch and later under English sovereignty. The brief chronicle of Sweden-Finland's colonizing activity beyond the Atlantic had been brought to a permanent close, although settlers from Sweden-Finland arrived on the Delaware even after 1655.[17]

Before turning to the later history of the settlers on the Delaware, the size and nature of the population in the communities which had thus become Dutch deserve brief mention. By collecting information from private letters and from official documents dealing with New Sweden, which are in the

17. Governor Rising's report of the surrender of New Sweden is printed in A. C. Myers (ed.), *op. cit.*, pp. 170-176.

State Archives in Sweden, Johnson has prepared a "List of officers, soldiers, servants and freemen in the colony, 1654-1655." The list shows a population, under this heading, of about 240 persons.[18] In July, 1654, Governor Rising reported to Stockholm that at that time the total population of the settlements was "three hundred and seventy souls" in all. This figure included more than twenty Dutch families who were forced to accept Swedish control after Rising had taken Fort Casimir. Nearly a year later—in June, 1655—Rising reported that the "Hollanders dwelling there [at former Fort Casimir] who took the oath [of allegiance to Sweden] are now gone off to Manathans, two or three weeks ago. . . . The land is now practically clear of the Hollanders."[19]

Assuming that Rising's figures are reliable—and there seems to be no good reason to doubt their accuracy—it would seem that in 1655 the total number of bona fide Finns and Swedes was in the neighborhood of three hundred. A few months after the Dutch had finally asserted their claim to the

18. *Op. cit.*, pp. 716-722, 726, and ch. xxxviii, especially note 45.

19. A. C. Myers (ed.), *op. cit.*, pp. 149, 164.

Delaware region, however, the Finnish and Swedish elements in the population grew considerably as a result of the arrival of new settlers from Sweden-Finland.

Before the news of the catastrophe on the Delaware had reached Sweden, preparations for another expedition to the colony had been begun. More than two hundred would-be colonists presented themselves, and from their number the most desirable colonists were chosen. When the ship *Mercurius* set sail across the seas, in November, 1655, it carried 105 settlers. The ship was in charge of Hendrick Huygen, who had been appointed head commissary of the colony. Huygen prepared a classified list of the passengers carried, which is unique in the history of the New Sweden colony. It appears to be the most complete record of any of the expeditions from Sweden as to the number of settlers, and furthermore it records the passengers in a manner that clearly separates the Finns from the Swedes. Huygen's list was as follows: [20]

Officers and servants.   9
Swedish women   2

---

20. The story of this expedition is told in Johnson, *op. cit.*, ch. xlix; the list is given on p. 634.

Swedish maidens   2
Finnish men, old and young   33
Finnish women   16
Finnish maidens   11
Finnish children from 12 years and
    thereunder   32

Total   105

After a voyage of nearly four months the *Mer-curius* sailed up the Delaware, in March, 1656. The settlers were denied permission to land, and the commissary, Huygen, was arrested. An appeal was sent to Stuyvesant, in New Amsterdam, asking for leave to obtain supplies and to return to Sweden. The decision was that the Finns and the Swedes were to remain on the ship, which was given free passage to New Amsterdam for the purpose of re-plenishing its stores. The passengers were dis-charged, however, in violation of the instructions sent by Stuyvesant, and once they had been landed, the Dutch allowed them to remain. The *Mercurius* was later taken to New Amsterdam and its cargo sold. It set sail for Europe sometime in the summer of the same year. By that time the newcomers it had brought to the Delaware had accepted—prob-ably with only few exceptions—the conditions as they found them and become settlers under Dutch jurisdiction.

After this addition to the Finns and Swedes on the Delaware and making allowance for some two-score soldiers and others who had left New Sweden when Rising returned to Sweden after his surrender to the Dutch, the total population of the settlements probably approximated four hundred. Of the total, nearly one hundred were Finns who had arrived on the last expedition, in 1656.

In view of the frequent mention of the recruiting of Finns for the expeditions before 1656, it seems reasonable to assume that they had constituted a substantial part of the population usually mentioned as Swedish before 1656. Population statistics have an unfortunate tendency to imply more than their real meaning warrants, especially when they relate to early times, when adequate recording was lacking. Estimates of population suffer from this defect even more, for as soon as they are expressed in percentages and the like, they seemingly assume a finality and an inflexibility foreign to the nature of approximations. But in view of the material summarized in this chapter, one seems to be justified in assuming the risks inherent in a numerical expression of an estimate and in saying that in

1656 at least one-half of the population of New Sweden was Finnish.[21]

Eight years later the number of the Finns was once again increased. In 1664, Peter Trotzig, the Swedish commissioner in Amsterdam, Holland, reported to his superiors in Stockholm the arrival in Holland of a group of 140 Finns who were on their way to the Delaware. According to Trotzig, the group consisted of men, women, and children; a few among the men knew Swedish. They had set out on the long journey from the region of Sundsvall, on the Gulf of Bothnia. Having sold their farms and other property, they had traveled to Christiania, Norway—present-day Oslo—and had taken passage there on a Dutch ship to Amsterdam. The emigrants appear to have been encouraged to leave for the New World by letters from relatives and friends living in New Sweden.

The authorities in Stockholm, believing that the Finns had been enticed to leave their homes by agents employed by Holland to recruit settlers for the regions from which Sweden had been ousted in

---

21. It is obvious, of course, that this estimate must be revised if and when new and more specific information relating to the Finns and the Swedes in Delaware is brought to light.

1655, instructed Trotzig to protest against the enterprise and to demand that the Finns be returned to Sweden. The protests and demands were ineffective, however, and in June, 1664, the emigrants sailed "for New Sweden in a vessel furnished by the city of Amsterdam; and the Swedish authorities were obliged to content themselves with requiring strict surveillance on the part of the governors of certain provinces in Finland to prevent such actions in the future." [22]

In the year when this last sizable group of Finns arrived in the New World, the English ousted the Dutch from New Amsterdam and from the Delaware as well. The later story of the pioneers in what had been for seventeen years New Sweden, falls therefore within the period when the English rather than the Dutch became the dominant influence both on the "South River" and the "North River."

---

22. Justin Winsor, *Narrative and Critical History of America*, IV, 486. Johnson, however, does not mention the departure of the group from Holland.

IV

RESOURCES

WHEN Klas Fleming and his colleagues made their plans for the New Sweden colony and superintended the various expeditions to the Delaware, mercantile interest was no doubt uppermost in their minds. The commercial objectives of the New Sweden Company were paramount; the settlements that were contemplated and later actually established were to serve the interests of the Company and through it the general interests of the mother country. But even if a predetermined economic system for the settlements was contemplated, little room was actually left for its realization. Because of the policy of neglect noted in the preceding chapter, the Finns and the Swedes were largely left to shift for themselves. They shaped their existence according to the demands of the new conditions of the New World.

To be sure, the governors and other officials were expected to administer and direct the colony in such a way that the men and women who came to the shores of the Delaware should serve the interests of the trading company. Even these representatives of the Crown, however, soon realized, especially in the early days of the settlements, that the basic needs of the newcomers were food and shelter rather than profits gained from trade. Unless the immigrants, who had grown up under conditions in Sweden-Finland that were markedly different from those of the wilderness found here, could adjust themselves to the new environment and wrest a living from it, the whole enterprise would be predestined to failure. The business of keeping alive was more important than the business of making a profit, and it forced at many a point less than complete observance of the instructions drawn up in the council chambers in Stockholm.

Under the system of close regulation and control, which was at least attempted and partly carried out, much depended on the ability of the governors. Of the New Sweden administrators, only Printz has left a record of achievement; Rising, the last of them, is worthy of mention primarily because he precipitated the events which resulted in the loss of New Sweden to the Dutch. The others are too-shadowy figures to deserve mention. Even Printz, one is tempted to say, has come to be considered outstanding largely because of his unusually impressive physique and because his predecessors were men of no achievement. Whatever his abilities might have enabled him to do under favorable conditions, the actual circumstances under which he was forced to carry on considerably reduced his stature. Against the combined effects of inefficient support from home and the handicaps which the limited resources of the settlements themselves imposed on him, even his autocratic nature and harsh rule could not prevent him from becoming, in the last analysis, a factor in charge of a trading post, rather than the administrator of a flourishing colony.

A sufficient number of colonists was, obviously, the most important single prerequisite for a successful colony. Colonists were ever hard to obtain, however, as we have seen. The attempt to solve the problem by sending to the Delaware lawbreakers of various kinds was not successful. It was only during the last few years of Swedish rule that voluntary emigration begins to be reflected in the meager accounts we have concerning the expeditions of 1648 and later. But even after that date, economically ambitious settlers were apparently not sufficiently numerous. Whether the absence of large numbers of colonists should be explained in terms of the inefficiency of the New Sweden Company or whether it should be considered a result of the absence of a compelling discontent at home, it is impossible to say. What can be said is that no unusual economic oppression or religious or political dissent is recorded in Sweden-Finland during the years 1638-1655.[1]

The New Sweden Company's monopolistic trade privileges may have acted as a deterrent to emigration; they limited economic opportunity within the colony and thus prevented the Delaware settlements from developing into a magnet attracting men and women desirous of reaching for the chance to improve their condition in the unknown New World. The few that came, were more often than not dissatisfied colonists not tied to the Company by bonds of common economic interest. The absence of individual economic incentive is forced upon one familiar with the story of New Sweden as one of the basic reasons for its failure to grow and to perpetuate itself.

---

1. In the course of the 1630's serious crop failures in Sweden caused much suffering. In 1650 and 1651 a terrible famine occurred, probably more serious than any in the course of the seventeenth century (Heckscher, op. cit., I, 404-405). It may be that the famines of 1650-1651 account for the growth in the number of persons willing to emigrate during the years immediately preceding 1655.

Whatever extravagant hopes of quick riches and great success may have animated the small band who landed on the Delaware in 1638 and the Finns and the Swedes who came later were dissipated by the experiences of the ensuing years. The first expedition was a financial failure, nor did the later expeditions, as far as I have been able to discover, bring profit. Fur trade with the Indians, the raising of tobacco—or its purchase from Virginia for purposes of export—and other means whereby the New Sweden Company attempted to make its venture profitable, all fell far short of bringing the returns expected.

In the reports of the New Sweden governors to Stockholm one finds several expressions of the thought that if only certain things would come to pass, or if provision could be made for this, that, and the other thing, success would attend upon the labors of the settlers. Thus Printz wrote in 1644 that "it is necessary that we have ships here again next December with all sorts of cargoes. . . . If this does not happen the Company will in the future suffer no less damage than it suffered in the past year, which cannot be repaired with 20,000 florins." Having referred in the same report to the facts that both the officers and the common people in New Sweden were desirous of leaving for the mother country and that provisions had been bought from the Dutch and the English in order to pay the salaries of the dissatisfied servants of the Company, Printz stated:

But if Her Royal Majesty and the Honorable Company should graciously decide to erect a trading-place and a shop with all sorts of provisions, small wares, cloth, and other goods, placing over it a wise and faithful man, who would have both that and other provisions under his charge and care, from which they could be given on their salary as much as each one should request, then the people could month after month be paid out of the gains alone, and the Honorable Company would probably retain the capital and a large part of the profit for its benefit, for everything is fearfully dear here.[2]

In 1647 Printz concluded that "if we had people, ammunition, and other necessary resources, we should not only be in a position to maintain ourselves in the said places [Fort Elfsborg, Fort Christina, and the fort on the Schuylkill called Korsholm], but also be enabled to settle and fortify other

---

2. These and the extracts from the reports of Printz and Rising that follow are taken from A. C. Myers, op. cit., pp. 93-165, where the reports are printed in full.

fine sites" along the Delaware. Rising, in 1654, suggested that security against Virginia and at the same time an opportunity to carry on trade with the Virginians would be achieved "if we only could buy" the necessary land from the Indians.

As we approach the fall of 1655, when Stuyvesant stepped in and took possession of the Delaware in the name of Holland, the "if" begins to sound a more ominous note, as is shown by the following quotation, taken from Rising's report in 1655:

I will now also humbly report concerning our present condition, namely, that everything is still in a fairly good state and especially since all here have the sure hope that a good succor from the Fatherland will soon relieve and comfort us, especially through Your Excellency and the assistance of the High Lords.

If the people were not animated by this hope, there would be danger that a part of them would go beyond their limits, or that indeed a large number of them would desert from here, not only because many necessaries are lacking, but also because both the savages and the Christians keep us in alarm. Our neighbors the Renappi threaten not only to kill our people in the land and ruin them, before we can become stronger and prevent such things, but also to destroy even the trade, both with the Minques and the other savage nations, as well as with the Christians. We must daily buy their friendship with presents, for they are and continue to be hostile, and worse than they have been hitherto. If large succors do not come soon we shall miss all our credit and respect with the savage nations, who will on that account insult us and do us harm. The Christians will also do us more harm than good, for we sit here as a beam in the eye unto them, and this work cannot be carried on with little succor sent at long intervals, for in that case it is as it was in the beginning, lost expense and work, and in the end it will all go to ruin.

But on the other hand . . . our courage [is] sustained by the belief that we shall indeed receive a complete succor, for we assure ourselves that Your Noble Highness and the Well-born Lords will not allow their work to go to pieces, which can become so great.

In 1647 Printz reported that "28 freemen are settled, and part of them provided with oxen and cows, so that they already begin to prosper; but women are wanting. Many more people [that is, persons employed by the Company] are willing to settle, but we cannot spare them on account of the places wanting them." He described the Delaware region in optimistic terms:

The country is very well suited for all sorts of cultivation; also for whale fishery and wine, if some one was here who understood the business. Mines of silver and gold may possibly be discovered, but nobody here has any knowledge about such things. The Hollanders boast that three years ago they found a gold mine between Manathans [Manhattan] and here, not in any place purchased by us, but nearer to New Sweden than to New Netherland. Hitherto, however, they have not got any gold out of it. There is no appearance here of salt, or of silkworms [because of the severity of the climate].

Lack of supplies was an ever-present problem, however, and even the trading activity of the Company left room for improvement. Referring to a report sent to Stockholm in 1644, Printz wrote three years later that

I mentioned the necessity of erecting a trading-house for various kinds of merchandise, namely, for clothing, shoes, different sorts of stuffs, linen cloth, thread, silk, fine and course cloth, divers colors for dyeing, buttons, Leyden ribbons, hats, belts, swords, tanned leather, etc. Those goods are very vendible here, and in Virginia and New England, and can be sold at a profit of 100 per cent. The house is also needed for all sorts of provisions, both for our own people and for foreigners.

By the 1650's conditions in New Sweden had no doubt been considerably improved. Indirect light upon the economic life of the colony is thrown by the following extract from Rising's report in 1654:

Besides timber-cutters, we need some one who can burn tar and make shoemaker's wax, which is here an expensive article; also a soap-maker, since we have a potash-burner with us. Besides this there are other materials of the land, which could be taken and manufactures, as saltpeter, for which we have a good man who can seek for it, and if we could here establish powder-mills it would bring us great profit. A powder-mill we could cause to be built on the above mentioned stream [one of the tributaries of the Delaware], but we should wish that skilled masters and people should be sent here. Of blacksmiths (aside from gunsmiths) we have enough for our needs, as well as cordwainers and leatherdressers, tailors, skinners, swordmakers, glass makers, masons, house-carpenters, etc. But we have need of potterymakers, brick-makers, lime-burners, cabinet makers, wooden-basin makers and wooden-plate turners, shoemakers and tanners. An assayer would be needed here. He ought to take the proofs and send them home as soon as the works had been started, in order that the neighbors, who have always tried to get up a copper mine, might not gain possession of one, but that strict orders should be given about it. For here are surely to be found many of the best minerals in the country. A French hat-maker could do much good here; also a winegrower and a bird-catcher who could capture geese and ducks in nets on the low places in spring and fall, since these birds come here by thousands in the fall and spring.

Even at that time, according to the governor, New Sweden was poorly prepared to withstand attack from the Dutch or others who might attempt to challenge Sweden's right to the Delaware region:

Cannon, iron as well as brass cannon, are here greatly needed by us, as well for service on the sea as on the forts, especially for the defense of the river at Trinity, where the cannon which the Hollanders left are mostly useless. . . . We have therefore borrowed four fourteen-pounders from the ship and placed them in an entrenchment before the fort, the better to sweep the river straight across. At Christina other guns are also needed, for most of the old ones are useless. We need a large quantity of powder and bullets, lead and other ammunition. Muskets and guns we have enough at this time, but good French fusils are much more used here in the country and in addition bags of leather with three or four compartments, in which one could place cartridges; these are many times better in the rain in the woods than bandeliers and match-lock muskets, and they are much sought after by the savages. We also intend to put flint-locks on a large number of our muskets.

Referring to the settlers who had survived the preceding year, Printz stated in 1644 that they have no longer any desire to remain here, but since I have caused some provisions to be bought from the English and Dutch sloops and given it to them on their request as part of their salary, they have had better health and have become more willing and have allowed themselves to be persuaded to remain here yet for some time. One observes, indeed, that it is more for the harm than for the benefit of the Company to give to the people here a part of their salary from those goods which have been bought to be used in trade, from which sum the gain will be subtracted at home, yet rather than that the people should leave, as has now happened, I have at all events thought it more advisable to preserve the people than to look upon the small gain; one sees that the amount and the damage are moderate and will not become in the end altogether too great.

Three years later, Printz again touched upon the many deaths which had occurred in New Sweden during 1643 and the inclination among the settlers to leave the Delaware:

The reason that so many people died in the year 1643 was that they had then to begin to work, and but little to eat. But afterward we gave them, besides their regular rations, board to apply on their wages, and they have done well from it. Still, all of them wish to be released, except the freemen [of whom there were twenty-eight at the time]. And it cannot be otherwise.

If the people willingly emigrating should be compelled to stay against their will, no others would desire to come here.

The soldiers and officers likewise wanted to be released from service. Rising also had to contend with the problem of finding food for the settlers and keeping them from abandoning the Company by flight. It is "unspeakably hard," he stated in his report in 1654, "to supply all this people with food in a desert [wilderness], yet if they lack anything they are immediately disposed to run away." It was in all probability the difficulty of obtaining and keeping settlers from Sweden-Finland that led Rising to surmise that "if some Dutch farmers could be brought here and settled on the Company's own land it would be very useful."

These extracts from official reports suffice to emphasize the difficulties with which the governors had to contend. They tell little or nothing, however, of the pioneer who constituted the real basis of New Sweden and who remained after Swedish governors and their reports and recommendations had ceased to play a part in the lives of the settlers on the Delaware.

The information that has come down to us concerning the daily work and life of the Finns and

Swedes on the Delaware is very scanty. We have no clear picture of the trade with the Indians, despite the fact that the record of merchandize brought to the colony is in many ways more fully reported than that of any other phase of New Sweden's economic life. We are almost completely in the dark as regards the multitudinous detail that constituted the daily round of the pioneer farmer. It is by inference rather than by direct information that we can picture the farming techniques which were used. Even more lost to us is information that would throw light upon the manners and customs of the settlers. The social side of their existence and in general those things that would disclose the manner of living seem to belong in the category of non-recorded New Sweden history.

Nor has much information been preserved that relates to buildings and the like. That is to say, even this relatively concrete aspect of the pioneering life of the Finns and the Swedes has been largely erased from the record. So too with the religious life. Several ministers served in the colony, but none appears to have left a description of the manifold duties which, one can guess, the minister was called upon to discharge. We know nothing of the sermons. That the Christian religion was to be upheld and preached according to the Augsburg Confession is recorded, but whether religious services meant services without proper vestments and ceremonial is not. The whole impact of the wilderness upon ceremonial, religious customs, holidays and the like can be only surmised, not measured. Not less elusive is the interesting problem of whether the ministers had any other interests except those of the cleric. Weddings, christenings, burials—did they represent informal and perhaps hasty incidents in the life of the pioneer, or did they serve as important festive or solemn occasions for the community as a whole? The answer can be formulated, it seems, only in terms of assumptions.[3]

Keeping in mind, then, that any conclusions concerning the extent of the "Americanization" of the Delaware Finns and Swedes (by 1655) must necessarily be tentative and general, the following may be suggested as indicating the trend of the times.

While the food and drink used by the settlers in daily life were undoubtedly largely determined by

3. The flimsy basis upon which attempts to describe these phases of life in New Sweden rest is clearly shown by Amandus Johnson's chapters xxxii and xxxiii, on "The Social and Economic Life of the Colony" and "Religious Worship and Ministers of the Gospel."

what the Delaware region had to offer—hunting and fishing played a significant rôle here as elsewhere—the customs of mealtime perhaps retained an Old World flavor for a considerable time. Clothing, footwear, style of dress, and the like soon showed the influence of the frontier, which ever tended to modify old ways of doing things. It is probably quite safe to assume that the Finns and the Swedes were about as successful in resisting the demands of frontier conditions as were their English and Dutch neighbors and that the pattern of life on the Delaware was not much different, once the necessary adjustments had been made, from that of corresponding settlements elsewhere on the Atlantic seaboard.

It was the Church that furnished the most important contact with the homeland and was the main agency in perpetuating the beliefs and mores of Sweden-Finland among the settlers. But it is unlikely that the Church ever became an anchorage strong enough to prevent a drift away from the old and toward the new. The religious life of the colony never developed to the point at which a Church could be said to have been formally established in the manner, for example, of the Anglican Church. No parishes were created during the Swedish period. The Lutheran Church on the Delaware was represented, as a matter of fact, by the labors and ministrations of a handful of ministers, and not by a definite ecclesiastical organization.

In general, the clergymen who were sent to the colony before 1655 stayed for only brief periods. The only exception was Lars Carolus Lock, a native of Finland. Lock came in 1647, served as Lutheran pastor on the Delaware for forty years, and acquired, among other things, the reputation of being frequently involved in trouble. If the Lutheran clerics in New Sweden included men of real spirit and vision, they came and went without leaving evidence of their achievement.

If we assume that religious customs were more tenaciously retained than others, the following statement by Johnson (page 543) may be accepted as a fair description of the observance of the main religious holiday among the settlers:

Many peculiar customs were and are observed in Finland and Sweden on these festive days, especially at Christmas, and some of these must have been practised in the colony. If a New England settler had visited the homesteads of the Swedes and Finns at Christmas, 1654, he would have seen much that was new to him. The floor of the dwellings were covered with straw, in some cases with finely cut spruce-branches; outside of some doors was a large cross made out of straw; a cross might also be seen on barrels and other vessels, painted there before the Christmas holidays, all for the purpose of driving away the evil spirits. The teeth of the cattle were often rubbed with salt and they were given extra feed on Christmas Eve; nor were the birds neglected, sheaves of rye or wheat being placed on poles for them to eat; steel was also placed in the barn and on the barn-door, that evil spirits should not enter. There was happiness everywhere. Long preparations had been made, special bread had been baked, special beer had been brewed and the best that the house could afford was brought forth. Candles were lit, especially two large ones for Christmas Eve and the clothes and silver of the house (if there was any), were brought in for the candles to shine on—it produced good luck.

We turn next to certain other aspects of the life of the Delaware pioneers, especially to those that relate to the business of tilling the soil. It is obvious that it was impossible, at first, to construct real houses. The early settlers probably were forced to content themselves with rude abodes dug in the ground, with the roof covered with sod, or to have recourse to simple dwellings of the wigwam type. Later the one-room log cabin made its appearance, and ultimately even more substantial houses were built. That roomy and comfortable houses appeared here and there is very likely, but they were no doubt exceptional during the whole period before 1655. As far as I have been able to discover, houses built of brick were nonexistent. Even the home of Governor Printz, on Tinicum Island, which has often been described as a sumptuous edifice, was built of logs, and was impressive, it seems, only by comparison with the unpretentious houses of the settlers.

Under the new conditions that the governors as well as the settlers had to face, the toilsome task of wresting a living from the virgin soil became the main business of the newcomers. To the task of forcing the soil to yield harvests, without which life would have been impossible, the Finns and the Swedes brought techniques familiar to them in the homeland; in the way of doing things, no less than in the manner of looking at things, the old ways had a natural tendency to persist. But new ways, better suited to the new conditions, were also acquired. From the Indians the pioneers learned techniques better adapted to the needs of a primitive existence in which the struggle against forest, swamp, and a climate as yet unfamiliar played a large part. In a word, the methods of farming in faraway Sweden-Finland came to be modified by the necessities of a simpler agriculture and, in general, of a more primitive civilization. Only to the extent to which this adaptation took place were the hard conditions under which the settlers began their life mastered and a permanent foothold in the wilderness gained. Ultimately, the pioneer farmer fell into step with Dutch, English, and other colonial neighbors, and he became fully adjusted to the new environment.

One of the farming techniques which the Finns and the Swedes brought to these shores stood them in good stead. As was pointed out in the first chapter, clearing land by cutting down the forest and burning the clearing was a general practice in Sweden-Finland, especially on the frontier of the older communities.[4] This method of clearing land was used on the Delaware, and in all likelihood played an important part in bringing land under cultivation.

The question of how much land the settlers were able to bring under the plow is difficult to answer. That efforts were made from the first to raise crops is known, but what the acreage cultivated by the farmers was in any given year is unknown. The evi-

---

4. Incidentally, Johnson (*op. cit.*) errs in labeling the Finns only as "forest destroyers." The Swedes knew the technique equally well, and practiced it.

dence suggests, however, that the acreage was very small. As late as 1654 the area which was under cultivation and owned by the New Sweden Company approximated only 325 acres. Regarding it Johnson remarks that "such was the extent of cultivated lands . . . when . . . Rising began to clear new lands in the autumn of 1654," and adds that by the summer of 1655, "this had more than doubled." [5] Assuming that this statement is correct, it seems that by 1655 some seven hundred acres represented the total amount of cleared land in New Sweden. It also leads to the conclusion that at that time perhaps no land was owned by individual farmers, title to it still being vested in the Company. Seventeen years of pioneering had thus produced results which were, as regards the growth of agrarian communities, exceedingly modest.

It has been said that "agriculture and cattle raising were now [about 1655] becoming of first importance in the colony." [6] In view of the facts mentioned above, this statement is probably an exaggeration as far as farming is concerned, nor does it seem to give an adequate picture of cattle raising. That is, the number of cattle in New Sweden and of

5. *Ibid.*, p. 527. See also the table on pp. 526-527.
6. *Ibid.*, p. 523.

livestock in general seems to have been small. Two horses and a colt were reported in 1640, and five horses, eight cows, five sheep, and two goats came from Sweden in 1641. Of these, two horses and one cow soon died. Pigs seem to have been more numerous from the start. Printz reported in 1647 that the colony had eleven cows and fourteen oxen and stated that because the settlers "need cattle as the principal instrument for the cultivation of the land, I intend to buy some next spring in Virginia." [7]

Referring to the close of the Swedish period, Johnson reports that the settlers "were well supplied with cattle when Printz returned to Sweden, but with the new expedition [of 1654] the cattle and horses became too few for the great number of freemen." But, he continues, in words that create a strong presumption that it is only too easy to overestimate the number of cattle in the colony,

When the English from Virginia, visited Christina in the summer, a contract was made with them for the delivery of a number of cows. Th. Ringold from Maryland desired to buy five or six mares. So large a number could not be spared, but it was agreed to sell two mares to him, each to be paid for by two cows that were with calf. In like manner March, who was the

---

7. Myers, *op. cit.*, pp. 124-125, and cf. p. 107.

richest man in his colony, promised to send over ten cows, when Ringold delivered his. Through these purchases the value of a cow in New Sweden fell about fifty per cent.[8]

As a matter of fact, the cattle problem appears to have remained acute to the very end, for Rising informed his superiors in Stockholm as late as July, 1655, that "since cattle are very necessary for agriculture, therefore I shall use all possible diligence in securing some here for the people." And he added, once again striking the "if" note mentioned in the opening pages of this chapter, that "it is sure that if a cargo were here of shoes, stockings, linen stuff, etc., then we could get as many cattle from Virginia as we wish, and could obtain them for a good price, and give them out or sell them to the freemen with advantage." [9] In the absence of the necessary cargo Rising had to provide for the future without the benefit of the profitable barter he had envisioned.

In general, the production of crops appears to

---

8. Op. cit., p. 523.

9. Myers, op. cit., p. 141. In the same report Rising discloses the lack of even competent fishermen; there are plenty of fish to be had, "provided only that a few good fishermen with all sorts of implements were sent here."

have meant a constant struggle with the vagaries of a strange climate, the destructiveness of insects, and the like. Thus Printz recorded in 1644 that

I planted last year maize all over, thinking . . . to receive yearly food for nine men from the planting of one man, but I received, from the work on nine men hardly a year's nourishment for one man. Immediately I sent the sloop to Manathans [Manhattan] and caused to be bought there for the company seven oxen, one cow, and 75 bushels of winter rye. And although they arrived a little late in the year yet I have caused three places to be sown with rye, also a little barley in the spring. It looks very fine.[10]

He expressed the hope that by purchasing corn from the Indians "the nourishment of the people shall not be so expensive hereafter as it has been before."

This dependence on the colonial neighbors of New Sweden is no isolated illustration of the difficulties that beset the pioneers. For instance, in 1655 the crops were so poor that there was no grain on hand for seeding, and a Hartford merchant by the name of Richard Lord was requested to deliver provisions and seed to the colony. In the preceding year, said Rising in his oft-mentioned report of 1655, "we could not have subsided with so many poor

---

10. *Ibid.,* p. 99.

people," if Lord had not come to the rescue. The task of supplying their own needs for food appears thus to have been hard enough to make it impossible for the settlers to improve their condition by exporting surplus products to outside markets.

During the first years of the New Sweden settlements tobacco was looked upon as a source of substantial profit, and efforts were made to cultivate it. As early as 1619 Virginia had exported some 20,000 pounds of tobacco and about 60,000 pounds in 1622. Realizing the value of tobacco as an article of trade, both Printz and Rising tried to benefit by it. The effort was a failure, perhaps primarily because tobacco, while it does not require skilled hands, does require many hands; the Delaware settlements never had an abundant source of labor, as we have seen. It seems that the attempt to grow tobacco was abandoned in 1647, for no tobacco grown by the Swedes and Finns was imported by Sweden after that date, although some "old fields" were planted with tobacco as late as 1655.

Frequent reference has been made in these pages to a category of settlers known as the "freemen." They were not independent, land-owning farmers, as has already been suggested. They were individuals free as to the person—thus readily distinguished from the indentured servants and others who came to the Delaware without enjoying full personal freedom—who worked for the Company and received wages in return for their labor. The wages were paid, in all likelihood, largely in commodities, from the Company's store, or the freeman received a part of the crop he raised. Money payment was rare. That the freemen were wage laborers is strongly suggested by several of the references to them in the reports of the governors. That they did not as a whole constitute a land-owning class can be safely asserted, although some of them probably owned the lands they cultivated.

It may be that by the time Rising arrived on the Delaware, in 1654, the absence of a land-owning farmer class had come to be considered an obstacle to the growth of New Sweden. At any rate, the authorities in Stockholm directed Rising to see to it that the land of the company was apportioned among the settlers, and his report of 1654 indicates that he was busy carrying out his instructions. Referring to the attempt to bring new land under cultivation, he stated that the task was made easier by the fact that a part of "the old freemen have requested new lands . . . and have wished to transfer their cleared land to the newcomers" who had arrived with Rising. But the new arrivals lacked the means to redeem the land. Rising therefore stated that he intended to buy the land in question for the Company:

(payment for only the clearing being understood) and then set young freemen upon them, lend them oxen for working their lands, give them grain for seeding, and each year take one-half of the grain from the field, and give them cows for half of the increase, on condition that if the cow dies before the Company gets any increase from her then the tenant must pay for her. By this means they are immediately and imperceptibly brought under a reasonable tax. So, if this gets started, they will both clear the land and supply it with cattle, and also give the Company a good income, so that it seems to me . . . that it could not be taken into better use, without any hazard, inconvenience or cost.[11]

Ultimately a number of the new colonists were settled, assisted to a start by the Company. It is not clear, however, whether the procedure adopted by Rising had results other than that of increasing the number of settlers from whom a tax in kind could be more or less readily collected. In any case, the régime of Rising was brought to a sudden close in

11. *Ibid.*, p. 139.

the year following, when Stuyvesant captured the colony, and consequently the position of the freeman appears to have remained virtually unchanged. It was not until after the English took over the Delaware settlements, in 1664, that a bona fide landowning farm class, enjoying legal title to the land, made its appearance.[12]

It must be abundantly clear, in the light of what has been noted in these pages, that the settlements which the Dutch took in 1655 constituted anything but a prosperous colony. In the course of the following decades, to be sure—first under the Dutch and from 1664 onward under the English—the regions which Sweden-Finland had precariously held

---

12. The attempt to aid the development of the colony by effecting new and presumably more efficient distribution of land among the settlers was not the only indication of a desire to infuse new life into New Sweden. Rising was also instructed to select suitable places where trading posts and villages could be established. Plans were made for the founding of a real town, with regular streets and blocks. It was also intended to found a staple town near Fort Christina. Manufacturing establishments of various kinds were to be started in the city, on which work was begun in the autumn of 1654. Nothing came of these plans, and when the Dutch forced the surrender of the colony in the following year, New Sweden was still without an urban community.

for seventeen years began to show real signs of growth. However, the story of this later period lies outside the limits of the present survey, which deals only with the period during which New Sweden remained a Swedish possession. Our chronicle will be brought to a close with an attempt to indicate the general significance of the colonizing efforts on the Delaware which constitute the main subject of our brief history.

V

APPRAISAL

EVEN a brief summary of the history of New Sweden invites an attempt to estimate, however broadly, the significance of the colony. Some aspects of the problem of formulating an estimate are so obvious as to require no comment, but others justify a summary statement.

How important was New Sweden for Sweden-Finland? Did it mean profitable exploitation, commercial and otherwise, of the resources of the Delaware region? Did it spell growth in the foreign trade of the mother country, a stimulus to industry, the accumulation of capital, the rise of a burgher class, the development of urban communities? The answers to these question and to others like them, have been given or partly indicated in the course of the narrative. They must be negative.

A recent Swedish writer says, in referring to the arrival on these shores of Peter Minuit and his followers, in 1638, that Sweden "had thus obtained a colony of her own, an event of great importance in the history of our country." [1] Similar statements have appeared time and again, particularly during the past year or two. They create the impression that New Sweden played a significant part in the seventeenth-century development of the mother country.

Evaluations of this kind are not supported, however, by the findings of sober scholarship. Thus, Eli F. Heckscher, the author of the most substantial economic history of Sweden that has appeared to date, fails to sustain them. In his study, which has been cited several times in these pages—the volumes that have appeared so far cover the years 1521-1720—he states that in selecting the materials for his volumes he has chosen the problems and developments most relevant to the conditions and trends of the period studied. Temporary developments and unimportant changes, he continues, "had to yield to that which seemed to be basic and lasting; frequently they are not mentioned at all." [2]

Accepting this test for separating the significant from the inconsequential, Professor Heckscher proceeds to give an unusually manysided and complete

---

1. Jacob Blees, *Svenska kolonien vid Delaware, 1638-1655* (Stockholm, 1937), p. 45.
2. *Op. cit.,* p. 7.

picture of the economic history of Sweden. In his history the New Sweden Company and the settlements on the Delaware are disposed of in about four lines, and the observation offered that the company is worthy of mention primarily because it illustrates the Dutch influence in Sweden, some aspects of which were summarized earlier on pages 23-41 of this study. In view of the weighty evidence furnished by Heckscher, one seems to be safe in concluding that the New Sweden experiment in colony building did not at any time play an important part in the economic growth of Sweden-Finland.

In appraising the place of New Sweden in America during the colonial period, one naturally turns first to the population problem. We have seen that by the end of the Swedish period the Finns and Swedes on the Delaware numbered about 400 souls and that the last arrivals in 1664 added some 140 Finns to the group.

As early as 1640 the population of New England was probably in the neighborhood of 25,000. At the time when New Sweden was lost to the Dutch, Maryland's population approximated—and perhaps exceeded—12,000. In 1664, when the English ousted the Dutch, the population of New Netherland was somewhat less than 10,000, a large part of which was English. It appears that in that year the combined population of New England, Maryland, and Virginia may be estimated at about 100,000. In the light of these figures—they are general estimates, of course—no labored argument is needed to make the point that the population of New Sweden represented only a small item in the colonial world of seventeenth-century America. The Finns and Swedes combined amounted to no more than about one person in two hundred.

That New Sweden and its settlers loom larger in the more limited history of the Delaware region is clear, however. That is to say, the Finns and the Swedes assume a greater significance in the early history of Delaware, Pennsylvania, and New Jersey than in the broader domain of general colonial history. For more than a generation before William Penn's time, they constituted the most important white element in the Delaware Valley. In Pennsylvania and southern New Jersey in particular they were the builders of the first permanent white settlements. The opening chapter in the history of Wilmington and New Castle, in Delaware, of Philadelphia, Chester, and other communities in Pennsylvania, of Salem, Raccoon, and other places in New Jersey—to mention only a few—must include, if accurately and properly written, references to the pioneers of 1638-1655 and to their descendants. This history, incidentally, is still largely unwritten; but signs are not wanting that it will be more adequately treated in the future.[3]

---

3. "The rewriting of early Pennsylvania history is the task confronting the Pennsylvania 300th Anniversary Commission, charged with commemorating the arrival of the first permanent white settlers of the Commonwealth under the flag of Sweden. For generations the tale of William Penn and the 'founding' of Pennsylvania, told and retold now makes it difficult for the average Pennsylvanian to realize that his Commonwealth had a prior civilization.

"It is a task primarily of education to convince people that a permanent settlement was effected upon soil later to become a part of the colony of Penn no less than 43 years prior to the promulgation of the Penn charter in 1681. It is important equally to recognize that a colonial governor functioned upon the soil of present day Pennsylvania no less than 38 years prior to the same date." From the "Foreword," in *The Brief History of the Colonization of New Sweden, Thereby Establishing the Foundation of Pennsylvania*. Distributed by the Pennsylvania 300th Anniversary Commission, in cooperation with the Pennsylvania Historical Commission and the Department of Public Instruction. The forthcoming volume *The Swedes and Finns in New Jersey*, ably prepared by Mrs. Irene Fuhlbruegge, under the auspices of the Federal Writers Project, should also be mentioned.

Even within the limits of local and state history, however, the period 1638-1655 is likely to remain partly unexplored. It is not until several years later that the sources begin to reveal, in some detail, the life of the Delaware pioneers and of their descendants. The emigration of a considerable number of Finns and Swedes to the New Jersey side of the river, there to lay the foundations of new communities, and the existence of those who remained on the western shore in the regions included in William Penn's grant, have left a record richer than that relating to the time of Printz and Rising. While the buildings—to mention but one example—before 1655 have been reduced to elusive descriptions, the houses and churches of the second and third generation of the Delaware pioneers have been preserved in a manner and to an extent that permit us to move closer to the period after, let us say, 1670 than to the decades that preceded that date. Swedesboro, Finns Point, Mullica River, and Mullica village, Steelman's Landing, and other places in New Jersey, for instance, reflect achievement in this later period. They challenge further research in the history of the people whose roots go back to New Sweden and through New Sweden to Sweden and

Finland, and will perhaps yield more concrete results than the original settlements before 1655.

In his *History of Chester*, published in 1877, John Hill Martin included a list of "Swedish families" living in former New Sweden in the year 1693. The list is based upon a document probably prepared by one of the founders of the Old Swedes' Church, in Philadelphia, who died in 1707. It shows 183 families and contains a total of 939 persons. The list probably does not make full allowance for the results of the intermarriage between Swedes, Finns, English, German, and Dutch elements, nor is it likely to include the Finns and the Swedes living on the New Jersey side of the river. The figure 939 probably furnishes, however, a rough indication of the size of the population element stemming from New Sweden toward the close of the century.

At that time, Pennsylvania's population was in the neighborhood of 10,000, and the total population in the colonies about 250,000. About one out of ten Pennsylvanians and about one out of 250 colonists in general may therefore, perhaps, be said to have been of New Sweden extraction. Incidentally, by the close of the seventeenth century the Finns apparently had become fully Swedish or English in speech, for there seems to be no evidence showing that any but Swedish services were held in the churches. Anglization of speech had no doubt proceeded far by the opening of the eighteenth century, and about a generation later English seems to have become the language of the majority of those who might still be considered "Swedes." The process of Anglization illustrated by the people in Penn's Neck, New Jersey, probably represented no isolated development. In 1741 the members of the local church recorded:

That since the congregation was now mostly English, they wished, after that day, to have their services always in the English language, and entirely give up their Swedish Church, to the service of the English people, in order that the Congregation be better enabled to support their teacher. . . . It was then decided that after that day no Swedish Service should any more be held in the Church of Penns Neck, but always English, with Prayers and Ceremonies according to the Church of England; which was also done.[4]

At the close of the Revolutionary War the American nation numbered more than 3,000,000 people. The extraordinary growth of the population during the preceding half century had submerged minority groups such as the Finns and the Swedes

---

4. Quoted in *Swedes and Finns in New Jersey*, ch. xi.

and had speeded their amalgamation with the dominant English element. By that time a few descendants of the original colonists on the Delaware had risen to local prominence or to more conspicuous service in state and nation. But the majority lived their lives as farmers, men of business, or members of the rising professions in that anonymous way which is the wont of the common man. Finn and Swede alike had become English in speech and American in manner of living, and New Sweden had become only an historical incident, largely lost in the greater, more compelling and more dramatic story of a new nation in the making.

APPENDICES

THE FOLLOWING APPENDICES HAVE BEEN INCLUDED IN THE PRESENT WORK BECAUSE THEY ARE DOCUMENTS THAT RELATE TO THE DELAWARE TERCENTENARY AND INDIRECTLY TO NEW SWEDEN AS WELL. NO ATTEMPT HAS BEEN MADE TO CORRECT THE MINOR HISTORICAL ERRORS WHICH ARE FOUND IN SOME OF THEM.

I

PUBLIC RESOLUTION NO. 102, 74th CONGRESS

H. J. Res. 499

JOINT RESOLUTION

AUTHORIZING and requesting the President to extend to the Government of Sweden and individuals an invitation to join the Government and people of the United States in the observance of the three-hundredth anniversary of the first permanent settlement in the Delaware River Valley, and for other purposes.

Whereas there is to be held at Wilmington, Delaware, and Philadelphia, Pennsylvania, and several places in other States, during the year 1938, celebrations commemorating the three-hundredth anniversary of the first permanent settlement in the Delaware River Valley, said settlement being also the first settlement of the colony of New Sweden, which embraced parts of the present States of Delaware, Pennsylvania, and New Jersey; and

Whereas, in accordance with a resolution of the General Assembly of the State of Delaware, approved March 20, 1935, the Governor of said State has appointed a commission of eleven members, designated as the Delaware Swedish Tercentenary Commission, with authority "to prepare plans for a fitting celebration by the State of Delaware on the occasion of the three-hundredth anniversary in 1938 of the founding of the first permanent government upon the soil of Delaware * * * ; and to cooperate with other commissions or committees representing the city of Wilmington; historical, patriotic, and other societies of the States of Delaware and other States; the governments of other States; and the National Governments of the United States and Sweden"; and

Whereas at its annual meeting held in Harrisburg, Pennsylvania, on January 17, 1935, the Pennsylvania Federation of Historical Societies (embracing seventy-three constituent historical societies) adopted the following resolution:

"Whereas plans are in preparation to celebrate the tercentenary of the landing of the Swedes on the Delaware and the establishment of the first permanent white settlement, and the first government in Pennsylvania, in 1638: Now therefore, be it

"Resolved, That this Federation pledge its hearty endorsement to such commemoration; and

"Resolved further, That the President be authorized to appoint such committee or committees to represent this Federation as may be necessary and to cooperate with similar New Jersey, Delaware, Swedish, or other committees."

Therefore be it

Resolved by the Senate and House of Representatives of the United States of America in Congress assembled, That when, in the opinion of the President of the United States, it shall be appropriate for him to do so, the President be, and he is hereby, authorized and requested to extend to the Government of Sweden and such individuals as the President may determine an invitation to unite with the Government and people of the United States in a fitting and appropriate observance of the three-hundredth anniversary of the first permanent settlement of Swedish colonists in Delaware, Pennsylvania, and New Jersey.

SEC. 2. There is hereby established a commission to be known as the United States Delaware Valley Tercentenary Commission (hereinafter referred to as the "Commission") to be composed of fifteen commissioners as follows: Five persons to be appointed by the President of the United States, five Members of the Senate to be appointed by the President of the Senate, and five Members of the House of Representatives to be appointed by the Speaker of the House of Representatives. The Commission, on behalf of the United States, shall cooperate with representatives of the States of Delaware and Pennsylvania in the appropriate observance of such anniversary, and shall extend appropriate courtesies to such representatives of the Government of Sweden, and other persons, as may respond to the invitation of the President extended as hereinbefore provided. The members of the Commission shall serve without compensation and shall select a chairman from among their number.

Sec. 3. There is hereby authorized to be appropriated, out of any money in the Treasury not otherwise appropriated, the sum of $10,000 to be expended by the Commission for expenses, including actual and necessary traveling and subsistence expenses incurred while discharging its functions under this resolution.

Approved, June 5, 1936.

II

75th CONGRESS 1st SESSION

S. J. Res. 135

IN THE HOUSE OF REPRESENTATIVES
APRIL 28, 1937
REFERRED TO THE COMMITTEE ON
FOREIGN AFFAIRS

JOINT RESOLUTION

To amend the public resolution approved June 5, 1936, entitled "Joint resolution authorizing and requesting the President to extend to the Government of Sweden and individuals an invitation to join the Government and people of the United States in the observance of the three-hundredth anniversary of the first permanent settlement in the Delaware River Valley, and for other purposes."

Resolved by the Senate and House of Representatives of the United States of America in Congress assembled, That section 1 of Public Resolution Numbered 102 of the Seventy-fourth Congress is amended by inserting a comma and the words "the Government of Finland" after the words "Government of Sweden" and before the word "and;" and by inserting the words "and Finnish" after the word "Swedish" and before the word "colonists."

That section 2 be amended by inserting the words "the Government of Finland" after the words "Government of Sweden" and before the word "and."

Passed the Senate April 27, 1937.

Attest: EDWIN A. HALSEY,
                               Secretary

APPENDICES

III

75th Congress   Report
1st Session   House of Representatives   No. 1391

FIRST PERMANENT SETTLEMENT IN DELAWARE RIVER VALLEY

JULY 29, 1937. *Referred to the House Calendar and ordered to be printed.*

MR. ALLEN of Pennsylvania, from the Committee of Foreign Affairs, submitted the following.

REPORT

(To accompany S. J. Res. 135)

The Committee on Foreign Affairs, to whom was referred the resolution (S. J. Res. 135) to amend the public resolution approved June 5, 1936, entitled "Joint resolution authorizing and requesting the President to extend to the Government of Sweden and individuals an invitation to join the Government and people of the United States in the observance of the three-hundredth anniversary of the first permanent settlement in the Delaware River Valley, and for other purposes," having considered the same, submit the following report thereon with the recommendation that it do pass.

It is proposed that an invitation be extended to the

[126]

Government of Finland to participate in the observance of the three-hundredth anniversary of the first
permanent settlement in the Delaware River Valley
because, at the time of this settlement, Finland was a
part of Sweden. It is therefore considered entirely appropriate to amend the public resolution of June 5,
1936 (49 Stat. 1486), accordingly. There are three
States involved in this celebration—Pennsylvania, New
Jersey and Delaware. Your committee has received
telegrams from the Governors of Pennsylvania and
New Jersey, asking that the law be amended so as to
include the Government of Finland in the celebration.
The telegrams are as follows:

HARRISBURG, PA., JULY 21, 1937

HON. SAMUEL D. MC REYNOLDS,

    CHAIRMAN, FOREIGN AFFAIRS COMMITTEE,

    HOUSE OF REPRESENTATIVES.

  MAY I URGE IMMEDIATE CONCURRENCE BY HOUSE IN SEN-
ATE JOINT RESOLUTION 135 EXTENDING TO GOVERNMENT
AND PEOPLE OF FINLAND INVITATION TO PARTICIPATE IN
DELAWARE CENTENNIAL. WILL APPRECIATE GREATLY YOUR
COOPERATION IN THIS MATTER.

            GEORGE H. EARLE,

            GOVERNOR OF PENNSYLVANIA

APPENDICES

THE NEW SWEDEN COLONY

Established in 1638; taken by the Dutch, 1654-55; taken by the English from the Dutch, 1664.

The source for the following statements is Amandus Johnson, Ph.D., the Swedish Settlements on the Delaware, Their History and Relations to the Indians, Dutch and English (2 vols.), University of Pennsylvania; D. Appleton & Co., agents; New York, 1911. The volumes are paginated consecutively and total 879 pages.

Dr. Johnson's book is the only large-scale treatment of the first settlement of the Delaware Valley. Dr.

[128]

Johnson is a Swedish-American, and has been the prime mover in the preparations for the 1938 celebration of the tercentenary of the Delaware settlement. Both the author and his work have come to stand for the most authoritative treatment to date of the subject, and can thus fairly be relied upon to furnish an answer to the question, To what an extent did the Finns participate in the settlement of the Delaware River Valley during the years 1638-55, when New Sweden represented on these shores the colonial efforts of the Swedish Kingdom?

I. Introductory

Before turning to the pages of Dr. Johnson's work for an answer to this question, it is essential to point out a few basic facts regarding Sweden and Finland.

Between about 1150 and 1300, Finland became a part of the Swedish Kingdom. By about 1350, it may be said that Finland had become an integral part of the kingdom. From that time on until 1808-9, when Russia conquered Finland, Finland constituted the eastern half of Sweden, not as a province but, to repeat, as an integral section of the realm. The inhabitants of Finland were on a footing of equality, politically and otherwise, with the inhabitants of the rest of the kingdom and were, as regards participation in the Riksdag, eligible to appointments to positions in

State or Church, "native Swedes" in the full sense of the word. During the period of nearly 600 years before the Russian conquest of 1808-9, law and the administration of justice, governmental organization, and educational and religious life in Sweden and Finland came to be institutionalized according to patterns which were evolved in common in the two parts of the kingdom.

These are facts that should be kept in mind in discussing those seventeenth-century developments in Sweden that relate to the New Sweden colony.

II. The Establishment of New Sweden

The New Sweden colony resulted, as was the case with most of the seventeenth-century colonies in North America, from the activities of a trading company. Both money and leadership for the enterprise came from the Finnish part of the kingdom as well as from Sweden proper. (See Johnson, vol. I, pp. 71-72, and cf. pp. 60-61.) Early in the enterprise, Admiral Klas Fleming, one of the leading members of the Finnish nobility, became associated with the New Sweden venture. From the first, he took charge of the affairs of the New Sweden Co., and served as the director of the company down to his death in 1644. Regarding the part played by Fleming in the New Sweden undertaking, Johnson gives a definite impression of substantial achievement. When Fleming died in 1644, Johnson says that "the company and the colony lost their best friend and most enthusiastic promoter" (vol. I, p. 230; see also vol. I, pp. 120-122-123, and passim).

III. Settlers in New Sweden, 1638-56

From the very first, it was difficult to obtain settlers for New Sweden. No settlers came in 1638. In the years following, recourse was had, from time to time, to the capture of poachers, deserters, and lawbreakers of various kinds. (See vol. I, p. 126.)

Among the persons condemned to serve in the New Sweden Colony were many Finns. Some of them had originally moved from Finland to Sweden proper—a considerable number of Finns had moved to the western provinces of Sweden after 1597—and had run afoul of the law by breaking hunting, forestry, and other ordinances. Other Finns came from Finland directly. (See vol. I, pp. 147, 239, 243; vol. II, p. 538.)

The colony remained small throughout the years it was under Swedish control. Johnson reports the following population figures:

Total number of male inhabitants, in 1644........ 105
Total number of inhabitants, in 1647.............. 183
Total number of male inhabitants, in 1648......... 83
Total number of "officers, soldiers, servants, freemen,"
1654-55 240

(For figures, see vol. I, p. 330; vol. II, pp. 710, 715, 716-722.)

Not a few of the settlers returned to Sweden, but it is perhaps safe to assume that these figures indicate in a general way the size of the population of the Swedish colony.

The question of how many of the New Sweden settlers were Swedes and how many should be classified as Finns admits of no fully satisfactory answer. Probably the outstanding reason for the difficulty is that the names of both Finns and Swedes were, as far as records are concerned, nearly always given in Swedish. Thus, Johnson mentions names like the following as belonging to Finnish settlers: Eskil Larsson, Klement Jöransson, Jöns Pafvelsson, Bertel Eskelsson, Clemet, Anders, Johan Mans, Clemet Mickelsson, Hendrick, Karin Lasse, Evert Hindricksson, Mans Jurrensson, Hinrick Matzon, Matts Hansson, Knut Martensson, Karl Jansson, Johan Fransson. (See vol. I, pp. 149, 150, 239, 463, 464, note; vol. II, pp. 535, 545, 547, 667, 712, 713.) Thus it is not easy to distinguish, by referring to names alone, between Swedes and Finns.

Both specific information and incidental reference in Johnson's study furnish, however, proof positive and final that the Finnish element in New Sweden was important. Of the 12 separate expeditions which were made to the colony between 1638 and 1656, only one is recorded in a manner that clearly separates the Finnish settlers from the Swedish. The last expedition, which arrived on the Delaware in March 1656, numbered 105 persons. Of those, 9 were officers and servants, 4 were Swedish women and maidens, 33 were Finnish men, 27 were Finnish women and maidens, 32 were Finnish children of 12 or under. (See vol. II, p. 634.)

Thus there were 92 Finns out of a total of 105. This figure of 105 takes on extra meaning when it is recalled that in 1654-55—the year preceding the arrival of the group of 105 persons—the total number of "officers, soldiers, servants, and freemen," which included a number of Finns who were in New Sweden already, was only 230.

In the absence of other evidence, it appears quite safe to say that at least one-third, and probably more than one-third of the population of the New Sweden colony was Finnish. This seems to be borne out by the frequent references in Johnson's work to the Finns in the colony. A few quotations will suffice to illustrate the extent to which Johnson, who in no sense attempts to do anything but tell the story of New Sweden as a whole, mentions the Finns.

In his chapter on the dwellings and customs (ch. 33) of the colonists, the very first sentence refers to the Finns, and throughout the chapter, the Swedes and the Finns are discussed in a way showing the importance of both or emphasizing customs and ways of doing things as being common to both groups. (See vol. I, pp. 345-346.)

In discussing agriculture in New Sweden in the 1650's, Johnson refers to an old method of clearing the forests by burning and says that "in Sweden and Finland this method became so common during the seventeenth century that ordinances were passed against it by the Government, many Finns being sent to New Sweden for violating these edicts" (vol. II, p. 528).

In referring to techniques of fishing prevalent at the time, spearing, eel-traps, etc., are mentioned, and the statement made that "the Swedes and the Finns came from regions where these methods of fishing were common" (vol. II, p. 537).

When Johnson tries to "construct a picture of 'social New Sweden,' " he states that some of the essential material for such a picture can be drawn from the account books, memorials, bills, and the like, but such sources, he adds, must be "supplemented by our knowledge of conditions in Sweden and Finland" at the time (vol. I, p. 164).

Finally, in speaking of religious and general church festivals in the colony, Johnson remarks:

Many peculiar customs were and are observed in Finland and Sweden on these festive days, especially at Christmas time, and some of these must have been practiced in the colony. If a New England settler had visited the homesteads of the Swedes and the Finns at Christmas, 1654, he would have seen much that was new to him (vol. II, p. 543). (See also vol. II, pp. 663, 665-670.)

IV. Conclusions

Even this brief summary, based upon the standard work in the field whose author has in no way gone out of his way to emphasize the Finnish element in New Sweden, justifies the following conclusions:

1. That the Finnish element in New Sweden was important; it represented one-third and probably more of the total population of the colony.

2. That insofar as the Federal Government of the United States takes cognizance of the tercentenary celebrations in 1938 of the first permanent settlements in the Delaware River Valley, its action should involve not only a recognition of Sweden and the Swedes, but of Finland and the Finns as well.

This resolution as reported is to amend section 1 and 2 of Public Resolution No. 102 (49 Stat. 1486), and in accordance with clause 2a, rule 13, there is inserted in this report sections 1 and 2 of Public Resolution No. 102 (with amendatory language in italics) which is as follows:

APPENDICES

Resolved by the Senate and House of Representatives of the United States of America in Congress assembled, That when, in the opinion of the President of the United States, it shall be appropriate for him to do so, the President be, and he is hereby, authorized and requested to extend to the Government of Sweden, *the Government of Finland,* and such individuals as the President may determine, an invitation to unite with the Government and people of the United States in a fitting and appropriate observance of the three-hundredth anniversary of the first permanent settlement of Swedish *and Finnish* colonists in Delaware, Pennsylvania and New Jersey.

Sec. 2. There is hereby established a commission to be known as the United States Delaware Valley Tercentenary Commission (hereinafter referred to as the "Commission") to be composed of fifteen commissioners, as follows: Five persons to be appointed by the President of the United States, five Members of the Senate to be appointed by the President of the Senate, and five Members of the House of Representatives to be appointed by the Speaker of the House of Representatives. The Commission, on behalf of the United States, shall cooperate with representatives of the States of Delaware and Pennsylvania in the appropriate observance of such anniversary, and shall extend appropriate courtesies to such representatives of the Government of Sweden, *the Government of Finland*, and other persons, as may respond to the invitation of the President extended as hereinbefore provided. The members of the Commission shall serve without compensation and shall select a chairman from among their number.

IV

THREE-HUNDREDTH ANNIVERSARY OF FIRST PERMANENT SETTLEMENT IN DELAWARE RIVER VALLEY

[Congressional Record, Aug. 21, 1937, pp. 12309-12312]

Mr. McReynolds. Mr. Speaker, I move to suspend the rules and pass Senate Joint Resolution 135, to amend the public resolution approved June 5, 1936, entitled "Joint resolution authorizing and requesting the President to extend to the Government of Sweden and individuals an invitation to join the Government and people of the United States in the observance of the three-hundredth anniversary of the first permanent settlement in the Delaware River Valley, and for other purposes."

The clerk read the joint resolution, as follows:

[137]

Senate Joint Resolution 135

Resolved, etc., That section 1 of Public Resolution No. 102 of the Seventy-fourth Congress is amended by inserting a comma and the words "the Government of Finland" after the words "Government of Sweden" and before the word "and"; and by inserting the words "and Finnish" after the word "Swedish" and before the word "colonists."

That section 2 be amended by inserting the words "the Government of Finland" after the words "Government of Sweden" and before the word "and."

THE SPEAKER. Is a second demanded?

MR. MARTIN of Massachusetts. Mr. Speaker, I demand a second.

MR. McREYNOLDS. Mr. Speaker, I ask unanimous consent that a second may be considered as ordered.

THE SPEAKER. Is there objection to the request of the gentleman from Tennessee?

There was no objection.

THE SPEAKER. The gentleman from Tennessee (Mr. McReynolds) is recognized for 20 minutes.

MR. McREYNOLDS. Mr. Speaker, I yield 5 minutes to the gentleman from Pennsylvania (Mr. Allen).

MR. ALLEN of Pennsylvania. Mr. Speaker, this bill merely amends public resolution approved June 5, 1936, entitled "Joint resolution authorizing and requesting the President of the United States to extend to the Government of Sweden and individuals an invitation to join the Government and people of the United States in the observance of the three-hundredth anniversary of the first permanent settlement in the Delaware River Valley."

It is proposed by the present resolution to include Finland in that invitation. That is all there is to it. It does not involve the expenditure of money or anything else except the invitation just referred to.

There is a good reason for doing so. Three States are involved in this celebration; namely, Delaware, New Jersey, and my own State of Pennsylvania. The Governors of the States of New Jersey and Pennsylvania have wired our Foreign Affairs Committee and asked that Finland be included in the invitation, and our committee favorably reported the pending resolution.

The background of this situation should be understood, because there is some opposition to the resolution.

Finland, at the time of this colonization, was an integral part of Sweden. Finland and Sweden were one and the same as far as governments were concerned, and the colonists who came to this country were composed largely of Finnish people. Like all the other colonization efforts of that day, this particular colony was promoted by a trading company. The admiral of one of the fleets that first came to this country was a Finn, Admiral Klas Fleming, and in one boatload that came 92 out of the 105 colonists were Finns. That was the expedition of March, 1656. Ninety-two of the total number of colonists were Finns, and it is pretty safe to assume that at least one-third of all the colonists in this little Swedish colony were Finns or of Finnish extraction.

Mr. Rankin. Will the gentleman yield?

Mr. Allen of Pennsylvania. I yield to the gentleman from Mississippi.

Mr. Rankin. May I suggest to the gentleman from Pennsylvania that probably that is one reason they are so willing to pay their debts, whereas other nations have refused.

Mr. Rich. I understand the State of Delaware invited Sweden to participate in this celebration and now we are trying as a Federal Government to have included in that invitation by Delaware the country of Finland. I cannot understand why the invitation should not come from the State of Delaware rather than the Federal Government taking action.

Mr. Allen of Pennsylvania. At the time of the original grant, parts of Pennsylvania and New Jersey were included, and in this celebration Pennsylvania and New Jersey are definitely included. It is not Delaware alone. The governors of Pennsylvania and New Jersey want Finland included and although we have not a telegram from the Governor of Delaware I understand that a Finnish delegation visited him and he expressed his approval that Finland should be included in the invitation.

Mr. McCormack. Will the gentleman yield?

Mr. Allen of Pennsylvania. I yield to the gentleman from Massachusetts.

Mr. McCormack. A State cannot invite the representatives of another country. That has to be done through the Federal Government.

Mr. Allen of Pennsylvania. Yes; and that is the purpose of the bill. In bringing this matter to a close, I want to emphasize the fact that we are going to celebrate the three-hundredth anniversary, of the founding of the first permanent colony in the Delaware Valley.

(Here the gavel fell.)

Mr. McReynolds. Mr. Speaker, I yield the gentleman 2 additional minutes.

Mr. Allen of Pennsylvania. We are inviting that little country that had a very definite part in the colonization of this territory, whose people played a prominent part and probably were a majority of the colonists. We are also extending the invitation to a nation that has been very friendly to the United States in recent years, and whose sense of honor and responsibility stands out above all others in the payment of its national debt to us.

All we are doing is holding a party, you may say. We have invited Sweden, and they should be invited. We want to extend the same invitation to Finland,

and two of the three states involved in this celebration have requested that we include Finland in the celebration. There is nothing selfish about it. It is not going to detract from the glory of Sweden in any respect. It is merely extending a little recognition to Finland.

Mr. Speaker, I sincerely hope when this bill comes to a vote I will have the support of all the Members who have a friendly and kindly feeling toward this little nation of Finland for what they did in the past and for what they are doing now. [Applause.]

THE SPEAKER pro tempore (Mr. Warren). The gentleman from Massachusetts [Mr. Martin] is recognised for 20 minutes.

MR. MARTIN of Massachusetts. Mr. Speaker, I yield 13 minutes to the gentleman from Massachusetts [Mr. Holmes].

MR. HOLMES. Mr. Speaker, I have no quarrel at all with my colleagues from Pennsylvania in their desire to include the little country of Finland in this three-hundredth anniversary. Personally I have nothing but the highest regard for that little country. However, we have here a somewhat complicated situation.

Early in 1936 at the request of the State of Delaware the House passed a resolution which was signed on June 5, 1936, inviting the Government of Sweden to participate in the celebration commemorating the three-hundredth anniversary of the first permanent settlement in the Delaware River Valley. This was done at the request of the State of Delaware. It is true at the time of that colonization the land which was first purchased from the Indians by the Swedes did include a section of New Jersey and Pennsylvania. The Government of Sweden naturally would not do anything or take any steps whatever to participate before receiving an official invitation from the United States Government.

When it did receive the invitation in August 1936 Sweden accepted and, as I understand it, the Swedish Government appropriated 350,000 crowns for expenses incidental to the preparation in Sweden and for expenses connected with the voyage to America. In addition to that, the Swedish people raised something like 250,000 crowns and they are at the present time carving a monument to be erected on a plat of land which was known as "The Rocks" in Delaware, where the first landing of these colonists took place. That monument will be here erected in time for the dedication in June 1938.

A group of Swedish-American people has worked on this celebration for nearly 30 years. Some 12 years ago they raised $450,000. The first step in connection with this celebration was the building of a museum in Philadelphia. During the last year this same group of people has received public subscriptions from the Swedish-Americans throughout the United States of over

$50,000 to help entertain the officials and representatives of the Swedish Government who will come here in 1938. In July 1936, a month after the original resolution was passed which invited the Government of Sweden, the Legislature of Pennsylvania passed a resolution asking the United States to invite the Government of Finland.

I certainly have no quarrel with the desire to have invited to the celebration the representatives of this splendid country, which has such a fine type of people, but I do not think it is quite fair to the Government of Sweden at this stage to include a resolution inviting Finland as a coequal of the government which was originally invited to participate in the celebration. Three hundred years ago Finland was a province of Sweden, and the two countries were under one flag, the Swedish flag. The expedition was financed jointly by the Swedish Government and the trading company, and the land was purchased in the name of the Swedish Government.

Mr. Dondero. Mr. Speaker, will the gentleman yield?

Mr. Holmes. I am pleased to yield to the gentleman from Michigan.

Mr. Dondero. I think it would be of interest to know how long ago the two countries separated. When was Finland divorced from Sweden, and when did it become a separate country?

Mr. Holmes. I cannot tell the gentleman exactly the date.

Personally, I feel there is more involved than simply the question of an invitation. There is also here a diplomatic situation which to my mind is somewhat serious. I think it would have been far better if the Legislature of Pennsylvania had directed its attention to one invitation, in view of the fact that Delaware had already made this request and the President had sent the invitation to Sweden. The resolution of the Legislature of the State of Pennsylvania was passed 30 days after the resolution here was approved. I think we are making a rather serious mistake in adopting this resolution today.

Mr. Allen of Pennsylvania. Mr. Speaker, will the gentleman yield?

Mr. Holmes. I yield to the gentleman from Pennsylvania.

Mr. Allen of Pennsylvania. Does the gentleman really believe it is a serious mistake to refuse to recognize the desire of the Finnish Government to participate in this celebration? They have expressed a desire to participate in this celebration, for Finland, at the time of the colonization, was a part of Sweden.

Mr. Holmes. I do not know that such a desire has been expressed by the Government of Finland. There are some Finnish-American people who have been very active in wanting to participate, but as far as the Government itself is concerned, I do not know that it has ever evinced such a desire.

Mr. ALLEN of Pennsylvania. The ancestors of these Finnish-Americans played a very important part in the colonization, and is only natural they would be interested in participating in the celebration.

Mr. HOLMES. That is quite true, I may say to the gentleman. The record shows there were quite a number of Finnish people who took part in later expeditions. However, there were a good many other nationalities who took part in the expedition.

Mr. DONDERO. Mr. Speaker, will the gentleman yield?

Mr. HOLMES. I yield to the gentleman from Michigan.

Mr. DONDERO. The complication in this situation arises not through any fault of the United States Government so much as it does from the failure on the part of the States which intend to participate in this celebration to request the Government of the United States to extend the invitation to Finland. I think this is where the complication arises.

Mr. HOLMES. Does the gentleman mean originally?

Mr. DONDERO. Originally; yes.

Mr. HOLMES. The gentleman is correct. However, the Congress passed a resolution at the request of the State of Delaware to invite the Swedish Government.

In further answer to the gentleman from Pennsylvania, I may say that I should like to see the United States some time honor the fine little country of Finland in some more outstanding and creditable way, and do it separately. Finland is the only nation which has met her obligations to the United States. She has demonstrated the fine type of her people, the quality of her people, the character of her people, and the honesty of her people. I should like to see some time set aside, when appropriate in the future, when that fine country will be the whole show and can receive proper recognition, and when we can pay Finland a proper tribute for being one of the most outstanding little countries in the world so far as concerns its friendliness to the United States in meeting its obligations, and its good will and friendly feeling for the people of the United States.[1]

MR. MCREYNOLDS. Mr. Speaker, I yield 3 minutes to the gentleman from Michigan [Mr. Hook].

MR. ANDERSON of Missouri. Mr. Speaker, I make the point of order there is no quorum present.

THE SPEAKER pro tempore (Mr. Warren). The chair will count.

MR. ANDERSON of Missouri. Mr. Speaker, I withdraw the point of order.

––––––––

1. Mr. Holmes made at this point a lengthy statement concerning the facts pertaining to New Sweden and the preparations of Sweden and Swedish Americans for the Tercentenary.

MR. HOOK. Mr. Speaker, in about 1350 Finland was an integral part of the Kingdom of Sweden, and then later, in 1809, Finland was taken over by Russia and later became an independent nation. At the time of the establishment of this colony there were a number of Finnish people who came with the Swedish people to locate in the Delaware Valley. During all those years the Finnish people were a separate nationality. They remained loyal to themselves and fought down through the ages until they established themselves as a democracy, and now they are a nation themselves loved and respected by all the leading nations of the world.

There is one thing that is paramount in that country, and that is the integrity they have kept with themselves throughout their entire history, the integrity they have kept with the world, and with this country today. [Applause.] It is the only nation that has paid its debt to the United States [applause], and in recognition of that fact alone they should be given a right to participate in this celebration. The sons and daughters of those pioneering ancestors who have adopted the United States as their home will appreciate this recognition, because they are rightly proud of the Finnish blood which flows through their veins. I have the pleasure and honor to enjoy the confidence of thousands of those people, and I know how loyal they are to honesty and justice.

There is no quarrel with Sweden. I have not heard the Swedish people say they did not want the Finnish Government to participate. They do want them to participate. Sweden is proud of the fact that at one time they were the owner of this wonderful little nation, and they are happy to have this nation participate in the celebration. [Applause.]

(Mr. Hook asked and was given permission to revise and extend his remarks in the Record.)

MR. MARTIN of Massachusetts. Mr. Speaker, I yield 2 minutes to the gentleman from New Jersey [Mr. Thomas].

MR. THOMAS of New Jersey. Mr. Speaker, I would like to support the Governor of New Jersey in the invitation to the people of Finland, but I support him for an entirely different reason than, perhaps, an historical one. I support him because I think the people of Finland should be invited to every celebration that is held in the United States. [Applause.] If there is one country in the world that we should invite to a celebration or that we should have a special celebration for, it is Finland. They are an incentive to the whole world, they are an example to the whole world, and they have certainly shown us that if there is one country in this world friendly to the United States, it is Finland, by having paid its obligations to us on the day they were due, and I hope this resolution passes. [Applause.]

[Here the gavel fell.]

Mr. McReynolds. Mr. Speaker, I yield myself 5 minutes.

Mr. Speaker, I am just going to say a few words in explanation. I feel there is no opposition, or very little opposition, to this bill. It was passed unanimously by the Senate. There is not much to it. Last year we passed a bill at the request of the States of Delaware, New Jersey, and Pennsylvania, to invite the Swedish Government to participate in this celebration, the invitation stating "and other individuals."

The Historical Society of Pennsylvania, through this act, extended an invitation to the Finnish Minister to participate, and he went down to the State Department and they concluded the language was not quite broad enough, and that is what brought the matter up.

When the bill came over to the House from the Senate we waited until at least two States had joined in the request, and they were the State of Pennsylvania and the State of New Jersey. They requested that the Finnish Government be invited.

It would be very embarrassing if we did not do this, and I hope the Members of the House will pass this little amendment. I know it will give great satisfaction to them and to the people at large who so greatly admire the Finnish Government for keeping their obligations with the American people. [Applause.]

Mr. Sumners of Texas. Mr. Speaker, will the gentleman yield?

Mr. McReynolds. I yield gladly.

Mr. Sumners of Texas. I want to join respectfully in the suggestion of the distinguished chairman of this committee. I am not sure I understand the resolution, but it seems to me under the circumstances, if we possibly can, this resolution ought to be unanimously passed by the House.

Mr. McReynolds. I really hope the gentleman from Massachusetts [Mr. Holmes] will withdraw his objection, so we can pass it unanimously.

Mr. Sumners of Texas. It ought to be passed unanimously.

The Speaker pro tempore. The question is on the motion of the gentleman from Tennessee to suspend the rules and pass the bill.

The question was taken; and two-thirds having voted in favor thereof, the rules were suspended and the bill was passed, and a motion to reconsider was laid on the table.

V

THE FINNS IN AMERICAN COLONIAL HISTORY

Being extension of remarks of Hon. Frank E. Hook, Member of Congress from Michigan in House of Representatives, August 21, 1937.

MR. SPEAKER, the House of Representatives has under consideration, through Senate Joint Resolution 135, an amendment to a previous act of the Congress which would extend to the Government and the people of Finland an invitation to participate in the three-hundredth anniversary celebration of the founding of New Sweden, the first permanent white settlement on the banks of the Delaware River. For my part I cannot imagine why this invitation, heretofore extended to the Government of Sweden, was not originally drafted to include the Government of Finland. Ascribed to an oversight, the Senate was quick to correct the deficiency. Today, on the eve of adjournment, we have the opportunity of joining with the Senate in passing this resolution authorizing and instructing the President to invite the Government of Finland to join with the Government of Sweden as our guests for this commemorative festivity. I hope the resolution will pass unanimously.

The year 1638, when the first Swedish-Finnish colony was established in the New World, was just 138 years previous to the signing of the Declaration of Independence, and, if we were to add 138 years to that eventful date, it would bring us down to our own modern 1914. As far back before the Revolutionary War as we are after it—this gives us a better picture of the sweep of the years since that eventful day nearly 300 years ago when these colonists of Sweden and Finland first landed on our shores.

In considering this colonial project, we must, of course, realize that Sweden as a nation was helped to its position of dominance in the affairs of Europe by the strength and virility of the people of its domain. Finland, then a grand duchy of Sweden, as over 150 years later a grand duchy of Russia, gave of her money and her people to the glory of Swedish arms. At one period of her history, in one of the destructive wars that militant Sweden was engaged in, Finland gave up one-third of her male population. Seventeenth-century historians bear witness to the valor and fortitude of the Finns.

According to our best historical authorities, this colonial enterprise of the Kingdom of Sweden, which encompassed the territory of Finland as a grand duchy, grew out of a proposal made to Gustavus Adolphus, illustrious ruler of the Swedes, by William Usselinx, a Netherlander, just about the time that the Pilgrim fathers were setting out from English shores for the wilderness of Cape Cod. The idea took, and the New Sweden company was organized on the 1st of May 1627, and the stock lists were opened to all Europe. The King himself pledged $400,000. The city of Wiipuri in modern Finland—Wiborg in Hanseatic League days—was a participant.

"Men of every land were solicited," says the American historian, Bancroft, "and it was resolved to invite colonists from all the nations of Europe. Other nations employed slaves in their colonies, and slaves cost a great deal, labor with reluctance, and soon perish from hard usage, so the Swedish appeal declared for free colony, saying, 'Surely we shall gain more by a free people with wives and children.' To the Scandinavian imagination, hope painted the New World as a paradise."

In the spring of 1638 the first ship from the Swedish Kingdom, the *Kalmar Nyckel*, arrived at the mouth of the Delaware River. It sailed up the river to the point where the city of Wilmington, Del., is now located. At the natural stone pier, still in existence and known as The Rocks, the small band of pioneers disembarked and thus began the effort which was destined to become the first permanent settlement in the Delaware River Valley.

The land upon which the colonists laid the foundations of a new pioneer Commonwealth in North America was purchased from friendly Indians. It extended as far up as the Schuylkill River, where Philadelphia, the cradle of our liberties, is now situated. Later additions to the territory of the New Sweden colony extended its boundaries so as ultimately to bring within its limits nearly all of present-day Delaware and sections of New Jersey and Maryland as well. Independence Hall itself stands on land that was one time a part of the colony, and in Wilmington the Holy Trinity Church—not to mention other churches in other places—harks back to these doughty pioneers of New Sweden.

In common with Virginia and the Massachusetts and other seventeenth-century colonies in North America, New Sweden on the Delaware resulted from the activities of a trading company. Both money and leadership for the enterprise came from the Finnish part of the Kingdom as well as from Sweden proper. Admiral Klaus Fleming, one of the leading members of the Finnish nobility, became associated with the New Sweden Co., and from the first was in charge of its affairs. His directorship of the company was cut short by his death in 1644. According to Dr. Amandus Johnson, the leading authority on this phase of American colonial history, "the company and colony lost their best friend and most enthusiastic promoter" when Fleming was killed in battle against the Danes.

The Finnish contribution to the population of New Sweden was likewise conspicuous.

While we do not as yet have altogether satisfactory statistics regarding the number of Finns in New Sweden, proof positive and final exists showing that they constituted an important element in the population of the colony. Of the 12 separate expeditions sent to the colony between 1638 and 1656, the records do not always clearly separate the Finnish settlers from the Swedish. The last expedition, which arrived on the Delaware in March 1656, numbered 105 persons. Of these 92 were listed as Finns. At the time of the arrival of this group the persons in the colony, presumably adults who included the Finns already in New Sweden, numbered some 240. As late as 1664 a group of 140 Finns were reported to have arrived in Amsterdam, Holland, on their way to New Sweden. A conservative estimate, therefore, places the Finns at from one-third to one-half of the pioneers of the Delaware River Valley.

To review further the progress of the colonial effort of the Swedes and Finns, which, incidentally, was but a scant 30 years after Jamestown had first been settled by the English, and but 15 years after the first Dutchmen had settled on Manhattan Island and founded New Amsterdam, we find the national jealousies of old Europe being transferred to the unsettled shores of the New World.

As Bancroft says: "The fame of Swedish arms protected the Swedish flag in the New World; and while Banner and Torstenson were humbling Austria and Denmark, the Dutch did not at first proceed beyond a protest. Meantime, tidings of the loveliness of the country had been borne to Scandinavia, and the peasantry of Sweden and of Finland longed to exchange their farms in Europe for homes on the Delaware. At the last considerable expedition there were more than a hundred families eager to embark for the land of promise, and unable to obtain a passage on the crowded vessels. . . . Philadelphia, like Delaware, traces its lineage to the Swedes, who had planted a suburb of Philadelphia before William Penn became its proprietary. . . . The Swedes and Dutch were left to contend for the Delaware. In the vicinity of the river the Swedish company was more powerful than its rival; but the province of New Netherlands was tenfold more populous than New Sweden."

And then the inevitable happened. A revival of Swedish aggression in the Delaware finally aroused the Dutch to action. In 1654 one-legged Peter Stuyvesant, who himself had arrived in New Amsterdam but in 1647, led a force of more than 600 men into the Delaware. Bancroft chronicles that "one fort after another surrendered, and to Rysingh, the Swedish Governor, honorable terms were conceded; the colonists were promised quiet possession of their estates; and jurisdiction of the Dutch was established.

"Such was the end of New Sweden," comments Bancroft, "the colony that connects our country with Gustavus Adolphus and the nations that dwell on the Gulf of Bothnia."

But although the Swedes had control of their colony for but 16 years the population remained. For more than a hundred years there was a direct contact between the Swedes and their church authorities in Sweden. These settlers—Swedes and Finns alike—retained their identity—linguistic, religious, cultural—but ultimately they merged with the blood stream of American nationality. Intermixture of Swedes and Finns and the anglicization of the language of both had proceeded apace by the time the fathers of this country created a new nation on this continent.

By that time a few descendants of the Delaware colonists had risen to positions sufficiently conspicuous to bring them into participation in the French and Indian and Revolutionary Wars as signers of the Declaration of Independence and, later, as signers of the Constitution of the United States. The majority lived the lives of hard-working pioneers and made their contributions to the development of American institutions and ideals in that anonymous manner which ever characterizes the life and endeavors of the common man who was then, as he is today, the real foundation of all that we hold dear and worthwhile in this glorious country.

As Bancroft, our own American historian, summarizes it: "The descendants of the colonists, in the course of generations, widely scattered and blended with emigrants of other lineage, constituted perhaps more than one part in two hundred of the population of our country in the early part of the nineteenth century. At the surrender they did not much exceed 700 souls. As Protestants, they shared the religious impulse of the age. They reverenced the bonds of family and the purity of morals; their children, under every disadvantage of teachers and Swedish books, were well instructed. With the natives they preserved peace. The love for their mother country and an abiding sentiment of loyalty toward its sovereign continued to distinguish them; at Stockholm they remained for a century the objects of a disinterested and generous regard; in the New World, a part of their descendants still preserve their altar and their dwellings around the graves of their fathers."

But let me return to the Finns. As we all know, there is one thing that Finland and the Finns have particularly impressed upon the consciousness of the American people. It is the integrity that they have kept with themselves throughout their entire history—the integrity they have kept with the world, and with this country in particular. Finland is the only nation that has fairly and promptly paid its debt to the United States. The citizens of the Finnish Republic have in these trying years, which might well be called an era of default and dishonesty in international commitments, followed a policy of honest dealing which excites the admiration of all who value the sanctity of contractual obligations.

In thus abundantly illustrating this all too rare policy of honest debtor, the Finns of today have only given relief to qualities that we find among the Finns along the Delaware centuries ago. Honesty, fair dealing, and hard work were characteristics of the Delaware Finns in the 1600's. We learn from a history of the New Sweden colony, published in 1702, that in a settlement named Finland, which was in the vicinity of present-day Chester, Pa., the Finns lived without fortifications, at peace with the Indians. Together with the Swedes they founded the first towns, built the first schools and roads, established the first law courts, and constructed the first churches in the Delaware Valley, and in doing so made important and lasting contributions to American civilization.

We who are celebrating this year the one hundred and fiftieth anniversary of the Constitution of the United States are likely to forget that just as the fathers of the Constitution wrought mightily, a century and a half ago, to lay the foundations of the independent United States, so these pioneers of the Delaware, some 150 years before the momentous Philadelphia Constitutional Convention, wrought mightily to carve organized civilized communities out of the wilderness.

The work of the fathers is being commemorated this year; the achievements of the Delaware settlers will be commemorated next year, in 1938.

It is my sincere hope that the Delaware Tercentenary, in which the Finns of Finland and our own citizens of Finnish antecedents will participate, will assume proportions commensurate with the importance of the seventeenth-century founders of the colony.

Let the tercentenary be celebrated in a manner that will clearly impress the American people with the fact that, according to history, the Finns were one of four nations that helped to settle the Original Thirteen States of the Union, the other three being the English, the Dutch, and the Swedes.

VI

THE AMERICAN-FINNISH ASPECT OF THE DELAWARE TERCENTENARY

NOT long after the Federal Congress passed an act, in 1936, authorizing and requesting the President to extend to the government of Sweden and to such individuals as the President may determine, "an invitation to unite with the government and people of the United States in a fitting and appropriate observance" of the three-hundredth anniversary of the first permanent settlements in the Delaware River valley, efforts were begun to include Finland in the invitation. In April, 1937, the Senate of the United States adopted an amending resolution providing for the invitation of Finland, and the House of Representatives did likewise on August 21, 1937. Acting upon the authorization of the Congress, President Roosevelt accordingly extended an invitation to Finland also to participate in the Tercentenary observance which will take place on June 27-30 of this year.

Especially after the action by the Congress, Finland and Americans of Finnish descent began to make preparations for the New Sweden Tercentenary. While some of the detail of the program remains to be worked out, at the time when these lines are being written (late April), the following outline of the preparations under way gives an idea of how Finland and Americans of Finnish background will participate in the official celebrations in Delaware, Pennsylvania, and New Jersey.

Despite the shortness of time, the people of Finland and the government of the Finnish Republic have assumed responsibility for an extensive program. Several months ago an official delegation to represent Finland was appointed. The delegation is headed by Dr. Rudolf Holsti, Minister of Foreign Affairs. Dr. Holsti is an authority on international law and lectured on that subject at Leland Stanford University in 1930. The other members of the delegation are: Vaino Hakkila, Speaker of the Finnish Parliament; Mauno Pekkala, Member of Parliament and former Minister of Agriculture; Arthur Leinonen, Member of Parliament, novelist, editor of the newspaper *Ilkka*; Victor Vesterinen, Member of Parliament, leader of the Agrarian Party; Miss Kyllikki Pohjala, Member of Parliament, nurse, leader among Finnish women, and former Rockefeller Fellow at Columbia University; Amos Anderson, former Member of Parliament, editor, and publisher; and Rev. Sigfrid Sirenius, representing the churches of Finland.

At the instance of the Swedish government the delegation from Finland will arrive on the M.S. *Kungsholm* on June 26, together with the Swedish delegation. The delegation from Finland will participate in all official events of the Tercentenary equally with the delegation from Sweden, beginning with the commemorative exercises at Wilmington on June 27, continuing at Philadelphia and various historic points on the Delaware River on June 28-29, and closing with the celebration arranged by New Jersey on June 30.

The sending of an official delegation to the Tercentenary is only one phase, however, of the program that Finland has adopted. A commemorative statue, sculptured by the leading Finnish sculptor, Väinö Aaltonen, will represent a gift of the people of Finland to the people of the United States, and will serve as a permanent marker of this anniversary of the common history of the two countries.

The statue will be located at Chester, Pennsylvania, in the proximity of which the seventeenth-century settlement called Finland was located. The unveiling of the statue will take place in the presence of the official delegates, representatives of the government of the United States, the State of Pennsylvania, the city of Chester, and of the many organizations through which Americans of Finnish background have in recent months mobilized financial and other resources enabling them to take an appropriate part in the Tercentenary. Finland is also issuing a special Delaware Tercentenary stamp, which no doubt has been released by the time this book appears.

Finally, celebrations in Finland on Sunday, June 26, constitute an important part of the program which Finland has drawn up. A huge festival is scheduled to take place in Helsinki, the Finnish capital, another in Rautalampi, the district in central Finland whence many of the Delaware Finns originally hailed, and a third in Vaasa, on the western coast.

Passing now to the participation of Americans of Finnish ancestry in the Tercentenary preparations, we note the following. For the past year, the American Finnish Delaware Tercentenary Committee has been leading and coördinating the work among them. The Committee has aided in the establishment of more than one hundred local and state committees throughout the United States, mapped out and conducted a necessary financial campaign, contacted and been in coöperation with the Delaware Tercentenary Commission of the State of Delaware and the Tercentenary Commission of the Federal Government, Pennsylvania and New Jersey. The Committee has in general carried on the effort designed not only to provide adequate participation for Finnish Americans in the Tercentenary, but likewise to make the Tercentenary in general as successful as possible.

The Committee, whose chairman is Hon. O. J. Larson, of Duluth, Minn., contains representatives from a large number of states in the Union. Three of its members serve, in various capacities, on the Tercentenary committees of Pennsylvania and New Jersey. Its honorary patrons are: Governor Richard C. Mc-Mullen, of Delaware; Governor George H. Earle, of Pennsylvania; Governor A. Harry Moore, of New Jersey; Governor Harry W. Nice, of Maryland; the Hon. A. K. Cajander, Prime Minister of Finland; and the

Hon. Eero Jarnefelt, Minister of Finland to the
United States.

Putting it briefly, the American Finnish Delaware
Tercentenary Committee has assumed a threefold responsibility. First, the mobilization of Finnish-American interests and resources for the benefit of the Tercentenary and the direction of the publicity work in
connection with the celebration. Second, the erection
of the monument which Finland and its people are
presenting to the United States. Third, the publication of a historical record which, while telling the story
of the New Sweden experiment in colonization as a
whole, will record more adequately than hitherto the
part which Finns played in it.

The generally accepted view of Americans of Finnish background as regards the meaning of the Delaware Tercentenary celebration is this. Three hundred
years ago, at a time when Sweden and Finland constituted a united kingdom and when Swedes and Finns
were equally subjects of the same Crown, Finns as well
as Swedes came to these shores and founded here the
first permanent settlements in what later became parts
of three of the original thirteen states of the Union.
While these Delaware pioneers at no time were as important in the development of the people of America,
as were their neighbors in, let us say, Virginia or New
England, their history does constitute a chapter in the
early story of this nation. Unpretentious though that

chapter be, Americans of Finnish descent see in it a secure anchorage which makes them more intimately connected with three hundred years of American tradition and therefore associates them more closely with the nation of today.

It is this circumstance among many others that has given meaning to the Tercentenary and made Finnish-American effort on its behalf a source of great satisfaction. It is this way of appraising the Tercentenary, that leads to the prediction that long after the Tercentenary has become a part of the past, Americans of Finnish antecedents will continue to enjoy the satisfactions which their work for the Delaware Tercentenary has already yielded in abundant measure.

INDEX

INDEX

INDEX

INDEX

New Sweden expeditions, frustration and failure of, 52; twelve made between 1638 and 1656, 132, 156; 1st (1638), arrival of pioneers, 3, 44; heavy loss, 49; Finnish element, 50; financial failure, 85; brought no settlers, 47, 53; 2d (Apr., 1640), delayed, 53; Finns among first real settlers, 55; 3d (Nov., 1640), colonists from Holland arrive, 56; 4th (1641), first appearance of real colonists, 55, 57; Finns who collided with law considered potential emigrants, 58; settle beyond Fort Christina, 59; 5th (1643), 59; Finnish element, 61; 6th (1644), 61; 7th and 8th (between 1644 and 1648), 62; 9th (1649), 64; Finnish element; disastrous voyage, 65; 10th (May, 1654), 66; 11th (Sept., 1654) sails to New Amsterdam, captured by Dutch, 66, 73; 12th (1656), 68, 76 ff.; only one recorded in manner that separates Finns and Swedes, 76, 132; Finnish element, 133, 139, 156

New Sweden colony, Dr. Johnson's book on, 128 ff.

New Sweden Company: established, 32, 38, 154; men responsible for formation, 40; cost of expedition to New

New Sweden Company (*Cont.*) World, 42; organization completed, 43; ships reach Delaware River, 44; land purchase, 48; hampered by lack of capital, 52; agreement eliminating Dutch from participation in colony, 56; commercial objectives, 81; financial failure, 85; acreage under cultivation owned by, 101; new colonists assisted by, 107; Fleming in charge of affairs, 130

Nice, Harry W., 165

North America, see America

North River, English become dominant influence on, 80

Old Swedes' Church, 116

Oxenstierna, Axel, 37, 39; part in formation of New Sweden Company, 40; director of New Sweden Company, 62

Paradise Point, 3

Penn's Neck, N. J., no Swedish service allowed in church of, 118

Pennsylvania: first permanent settlements, 59; Finns and Swedes builders of first permanent settlements, 113, 114 n., 115; population, 116; tercentenary celebration of first permanent settlement on Delaware, 123, 127, 139, 140, 150, 162; requests that Finland be invited to participate in tercentenary celebration, 144, 150

INDEX

INDEX

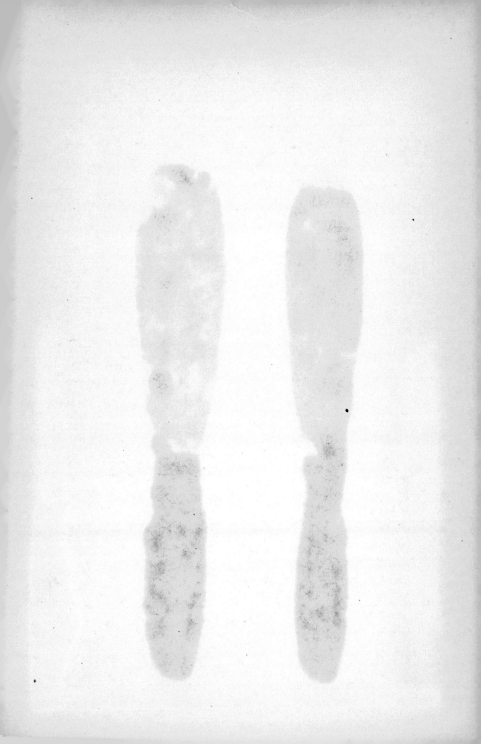

DATE DUE

GAYLORD   PRINTED IN U.S.A.